Canadian Pacific
In Color
VOLUME 2: *Western Lines*
BILL LINLEY

Copyright © 2011
Morning Sun Books, Inc.
All rights reserved. This book may not be reproduced in part or in whole without written permission from the publisher, except in the case of brief quotations or reproductions of the cover for the purposes of review.

Published by
Morning Sun Books, Inc.
9 Pheasant Lane
Scotch Plains, NJ 07076
Printed in Korea

Library of Congress
Catalog Card No. 2002106741

First Printing
ISBN 1-58248-313-2

To access our full library *In Color* visit us at
www.morningsunbooks.com

ROBERT J. YANOSEY, President

DEDICATION
For Judy (Smith) Linley
December 15, 1949 – September 13, 2005
My soul mate, mother to our daughters Sarah and Rachel, and inspiration for my books
on the Canadian Pacific Railway

Left ◉ Judy prepares to photograph chartered RDC-1 9049 (ex DSS&A 500) in Ottawa, Ontario as it makes a runpast for guests aboard *The Matrimonial* on our wedding day, Saturday, May 26, 1973. *(Bill Linley)*

ACKNOWLEDGEMENTS
This second volume of images of the Canadian Pacific Railway has been long delayed as motivation waned with the lengthy illness and passing of my first wife, Judy. To all of those who encouraged me to complete this work, I am extremely grateful. I trust that their confidence will be rewarded in the assembled photographs and supporting material.

Credit is particularly due to my lifelong friend George Melvin of Readfield, Maine for our late night conversation while driving in the Colorado Rockies in 1996 that led directly to my Morning Sun books on the Canadian Pacific. I am indebted to George and his wife, Kathy, for persistent encouragement during earlier bleak times to bring these images to print. Other lifelong friends including Bruce Chapman, Gerry Gaugl, Ken McCutcheon, David Morris and Earl Roberts have also made numerous contributions. Significant input was received from friends old and new including David Ames, Fred Angus, Andrew Cassidy, Peter Cox, Steven Dickie, D'Arcy Furlonger, Ken Goslett, Ross Harrison, Fred Headon, Bill Hooper, Jim Johnston, Ray Kennedy, Les Kozma, John Lachance, Peter Leyland, Bob Loat, Ray Matthews, David Othen, Mark Perry, Doug Phillips, Jeff Pinchbeck, George Pitarys, Andrew Renaud, Ron Ritchie, Sean Robitaille, Glenn Roemer, John Rushton, Bob Sandusky, Brian Schuff, Stan Smaill, David Stremes, Ted Wickson and Dale Wilson. Marilynn Linley's support and encouragement is deeply appreciated.

I appreciate the trackside hours enjoyed by all of the photographers who are credited elsewhere in this book.

Readers are encouraged to further examine the many sources that I have referenced for this volume. Important among these are *Canadian Pacific Steam Locomotives* by Omer Lavallee; *Canadian Pacific Diesel Locomotives* by Murrary Dean and David Hanna; *Canadian Pacific's Western Depots* by Charles Bohi and Leslie Kozma; *The Crow and the Kettle* by John Garden; *Lines of Country: An Atlas of Railway and Waterway History in Canada* by Christopher Andreae; *Railway Mileposts: British Columbia,* two volumes by Roger Burrows; *Kettle Valley Railway Mileboards* by Joe Smuin; *The Pacific Princesses* and *The Pacific Empresses* by Robert Turner; *Trackside Guides* edited by Earl Roberts and David Stremes; and various volumes published by the late Donald Bain of the B.R.M.N.A. in Calgary.

Once again, I am indebted to Bob Yanosey of Morning Sun Books for his dedication to the task of bringing vintage color images to print.

Bill Linley, Halifax, Nova Scotia, May 2010

Table of Contents

Great Lakes Steamships 9	REVELSTOKE DIVISION 87
PRARIE REGION 12	Windermere Sub 87
FORT WILLIAM DIVISION 12	Mountain Sub 88
Kaministiquia Sub 12	Shuswap Sub 96
Ignace Sub 15	Okanagan Sub 101
Keewatin Sub 16	Osoyoos Sub 102
Lac du Bonnet Sub 18	CANYON DIVISION 103
Emerson Sub 19	Thompson Sub 103
Winnipeg Beach Sub 20	Princeton Sub 104
WINNIPEG TERMINAL DIVISION 21	Mission Sub 106
BRANDON DIVISION 27	Cascade Sub 106
Glenboro Sub 27	VANCOUVER DIVISION 108
Carberry Sub 28	Cascade Sub 108
Broadview Sub 29	Westminster Sub 113
Miniota Sub 32	E & N DIVISION 114
Neudorf Sub 32	Victoria Sub 114
Bredenbury Sub 33	KOOTENAY DIVISION 118
Estevan Sub 34	Cranbrook Sub 118
REGINA DIVISION 35	Kimberley Sub 119
Indian Head Sub 35	Kingsgate Sub 119
Lanigan Sub 38	Nelson Sub 120
Portal Sub 39	Boundary Sub 122
Bromhead Sub 41	Carmi Sub 124
MOOSE JAW DIVISION 42	Rossland Sub 124
Outlook Sub 42	Slocan Sub 126
Swift Current Sub 44	Kaslo Sub 127
Shaunavon Sub 49	Arrow Lakes 128
SASKATOON DIVISION 50	
Wynyard Sub 50	
Sutherland Sub 51	
Prince Albert Sub 51	
Wilkie Sub 52	
Cutknife Sub 53	
Meadow Lake Sub 54	
PACIFIC REGION 56	
MEDICINE HAT DIVISION 56	
Maple Creek Sub 56	
Brooks Sub 57	
Langdon Sub 59	
Empress Sub 59	
Bassano Sub 60	
Irricana Sub 60	
EDMONTON DIVISION 61	
Leduc Sub 61	
CALGARY DIVISION 63	
Red Deer Sub 63	
Calgary Terminals 66	
Laggan Sub 71	
LETHBRIDGE DIVISION 81	
Taber Sub 81	
Crowsnest Sub 81	
Aldersyde Sub 84	
MacLeod Sub 85	

Above & Page One ◉ "Tall and long." Train Master 8917 rests at the Alyth Diesel Shop on Monday, September 23, 1968.
(Bill Linley)

Canadian Pacific In Color

Canadian Pacific *In Color*
Western Lines
Volume 2

Welcome to *Canadian Pacific in Color Volume II: Western Lines*. This volume continues the illustrated story of the Canadian Pacific Railway's operations from 1949 through 1968, a colorful period marked by the transition from steam to diesel motive power, concluding with the retirement of the tuscan and grey corporate image. The 1,892 miles from Fort William to Vancouver were the umbilical cord of the Company's western operations collectively known prior to 1960 as the Western Lines.

SPANS THE WORLD

Incorporated in February 1881, the Canadian Pacific Railway Company (CPR) contracted with the Government of Canada to complete the latter's promise of 1871 to build a railway from Montreal to the Pacific Coast. With a $25 million construction subsidy and a 25-million acre land grant, the CPR was able to begin construction of the transcontinental railway. Market conditions led to the near collapse of the Company in 1884-85, however, these were overcome and the contract was completed on November 7, 1885. Increasing prosperity was enjoyed as settlers moved to the West, particularly after 1896.

The "Crow Rate" enshrined in perpetuity reductions in the freight rates of 1897 for the westward movement of settlers' effects and for the eastbound movement of unprocessed grains and flour to Fort William. In exchange, the CPR gained a $3.6 million subsidy, earned a land grant of 3.7 million acres, and accessed the rich mineral traffic west of the Crowsnest Pass in southeastern British Columbia. The rate was modified but not increased in 1927 to exclude settlers' effects and flour traffic, but was extended to all of the Company's lines. Thereafter, the "Crow" became increasingly burdensome as it grew to as much as 47% of traffic carried in mid-century, its profitability ebbed, and equipment replacement and service issues were created.

Prior to World War I, the Company developed 4,212 miles of branchlines throughout the Prairies. Mainlines reached Saskatoon and Edmonton and much of the 1,250-mile line from Fort William to Calgary was double-tracked. Other enhancements to the route in British Columbia included the Spiral Tunnels (1909) replacing the steeply graded line on the western approach to Kicking Horse Pass as well as the Connaught Tunnel (1916) at the summit of Rogers Pass. Construction continued through the 1920's; thereafter, new lines were mostly intended to access industrial sites.

The Company's network of hotels in Western Canada was established prior to World War I and included the Empress in Victoria, a new Hotel Vancouver, the Palliser in Calgary and the Royal Alexandra in Winnipeg. In the western mountains, the Banff Springs Hotel, the Chateau Lake Louise, Mount Stephen House and Glacier House attracted numerous guests most of whom arrived on CPR trains until mid-century. The Hotel Saskatchewan was opened in Regina in 1927. Land development on the Prairies was highlighted by significant land sales and by the creation of the Irrigation Block southeast of Calgary where almost 600,000 acres were irrigated by 1914. Later in the same year, the Department of Natural Resources, headquartered in Calgary, pioneered the development of the petroleum industry based initially on the Company's retention of mineral rights on lands that it had sold. The Trail smelter was acquired in 1898 and parlayed into the large Cominco lead-zinc refining operation as the decades progressed.

The Canadian Pacific Coast Steamship Service started in 1901 with the acquisition of the privately owned Canadian Pacific Navigation Company that began operations along the British Columbia Coast in 1883. A fleet of vessels named *"Princesses"* plied the Pacific waters between Seattle and Skagway. The main service, the Triangle Route linking Vancouver, Victoria and Seattle, featured daytime and overnight services prior to 1949. By the 1950's, the wartime loss of the first *Princess Margeurite*, aging vessels unsuited to the movement of automobile focused travel, competition from the provincially owned B.C. Ferries, as well as the Blackball Line of Seattle on the main routes from the Lower Mainland to Vancouver Island, all led to some new vessel construction and gradual service reductions. By October 1962, the remaining vessels were the *Princess Patricia* (1948) on Alaskan Cruises, a replacement *Princess Margeurite* (1948) linking Victoria and Seattle, and the *Princess of Vancouver* (1955) serving the Vancouver – Nanaimo route. The *Trailer Princess*, essentially a self-propelled transfer barge, was added in 1966 to enhance truck and railcar service to Nanaimo.

Coincident with the start of transcontinental service in the summer of 1886, the CPR sought to develop its traffic by establishing shipping routes across the Pacific to Japan, China, Hong Kong and the Philippines. Chartered sailing ships were quickly replaced with a trio of elderly steamships followed by three ships newly constructed in England for the CPR following the awarding of a mail contract. Six larger and faster *Empresses* constructed through 1930 followed the first *Empresses of India, Japan and China* of 1891 and provided service on the North Pacific until 1941. Only one of the four Pacific Empresses survived World War II, the *Empress of Scotland*, formerly the *Empress of Japan* (II). She was assigned to service on the North Atlantic leaving only the *Aorangi* of the Canadian Australasian Line, in which the CPR shared equal ownership with the Union Steamship Company of New Zealand, to resume service on the South Pacific to Auckland and Sydney in 1948. The service struggled with a meagre subsidy and was finally closed in May 1953.

The replacement for the *Empresses* was to be the similarly named aircraft of the Canadian Pacific Air Lines. Beginning with the purchase of existing regional and charter carriers, notably in Western Canada and the North, the airline was established in 1942. International routes to China, Japan and Australia began in 1949 and cross-Canada service in 1959. Additional routes from Vancouver, Montreal or Toronto reached Amsterdam, Southern Europe, South America and Mexico. Regional operations were concentrated in British Columbia, Alberta and the Yukon. By 1968, the company had embraced Douglas DC-8 and Boeing 737 jets and had gained federal government authorization to provide 25% of the available seats on the lucrative Montreal – Toronto – Vancouver route.

The growth in the railway, hotels, shipping and airlines and supporting resource industries gave continuing truth to the corporate slogan of the late 1940's: "Spans The World."

Below ⊕ *B.C. Coast Steamships menu of 1953 featuring* Princesses Patricia and Margeurite, *GMDL F units and the de Havilland Comet 1's then on order.* (Gerry Gaugl Collection)

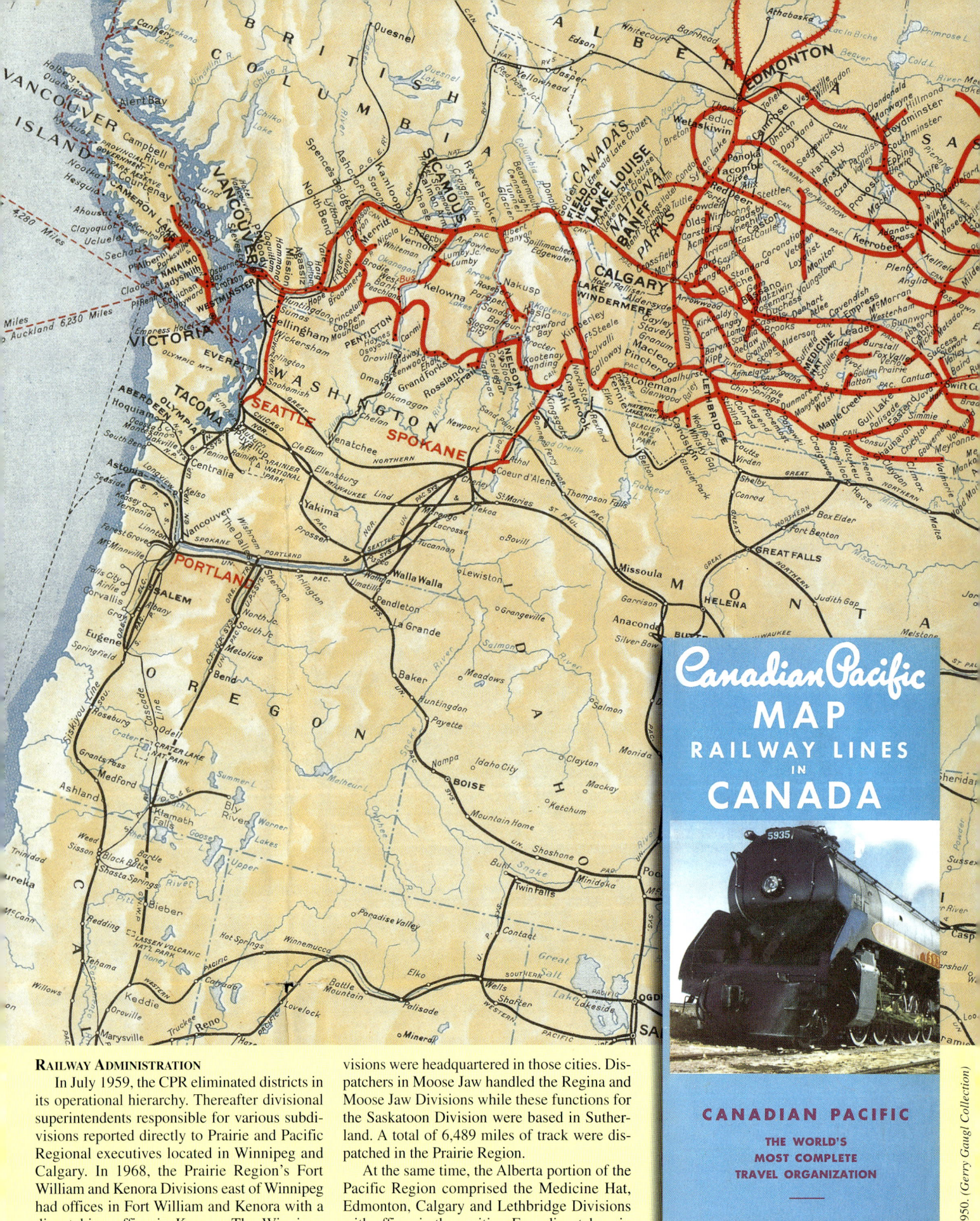

RAILWAY ADMINISTRATION

In July 1959, the CPR eliminated districts in its operational hierarchy. Thereafter divisional superintendents responsible for various subdivisions reported directly to Prairie and Pacific Regional executives located in Winnipeg and Calgary. In 1968, the Prairie Region's Fort William and Kenora Divisions east of Winnipeg had offices in Fort William and Kenora with a dispatching office in Kenora. The Winnipeg Terminal and Brandon divisions were headquartered in their respective cities with the dispatching office in Brandon. The Regina, Moose Jaw and Saskatoon Divisions were headquartered in those cities. Dispatchers in Moose Jaw handled the Regina and Moose Jaw Divisions while these functions for the Saskatoon Division were based in Sutherland. A total of 6,489 miles of track were dispatched in the Prairie Region.

At the same time, the Alberta portion of the Pacific Region comprised the Medicine Hat, Edmonton, Calgary and Lethbridge Divisions with offices in those cities. Four dispatchers in Calgary controlled 2,996 miles of track. In British Columbia, the Revelstoke Division was dispatched from the divisional office in Revelstoke. The Canyon and Vancouver Divisions

were headquartered and dispatched from offices in Vancouver. The E and N Division had offices and a dispatcher in Victoria. Finally, the Kootenay Division and its dispatchers were based in Nelson. 1,925 miles of track were dispatched from locations in British Columbia. It should be noted that the organization of this book follows that of the subdivision listings in the four employee timetables for the Western Lines from October 1968.

Railway operations were governed by Standard Time throughout the year although passenger timetables after April 28, 1968 followed the public convention of the seasonal switch to and from Daylight Saving Time. Until October 27, 1968, and uniquely to the Western Lines, operations dispensed with the a.m. and p.m. notations in favour of a four-digit, 24-hour clock beginning at 01.00 in the morning. Hence, operating timetables included references to times such as 01.50 and 24.45.

MOTIVE POWER ON THE WESTERN LINES

At the end of December 1952 the Western Lines rostered 864 steam engines, over 53% of those on the system at that time. The largest groupings were the 209 Pacifics, 181 Mikados and 179 Ten-Wheelers. Of the 80 ten-coupled engines rostered, all but six Decapods were assigned to the Western Lines. Engines were assigned at 45 locations, although the ten largest terminals accounted for more than two-thirds of the engines. Winnipeg was home to 104 engines, Calgary (Alyth) 82, and Moose Jaw 68, while seven terminals including Ignace, Fort MacLeod and Sicamous housed just one locomotive.

The initial use of diesels in the West was in September 1944 when Alco S-2 switchers 7015 – 7017 were delivered to Winnipeg and 7018 and 7019 went to work in Calgary. Dieselization of yards on the Western Lines proceeded

Volume 2 · 5

more slowly than in the East, so 63% of all steam switchers were in the West in 1952. Over the years, DS4-4-1000, S-2, S-3, S-4, SW8, SW9 and SW900 models were added to Western Lines terminals to replace steam switchers concluding with eight MLW S-10 units in 1958.

The CPR's initial study of dieselization was undertaken in 1947 on the E and N Division on Vancouver Island whose self-contained nature would best demonstrate the potential benefits of the complete replacement of steam engines. Ultimately thirteen DRS4-4-1000 road switchers replaced 20 steamers on the Island and eleven DS4-4-1000 switchers went to Vancouver. Due to material shortages the Baldwins were acquired in lieu of additional Alco or EMD locomotives. Their construction at Eddystone, PA was contracted through the Canadian Locomotive Company of Kingston, Ontario. Between 1957 and 1968 the Baldwins were equipped with MU controls and operated on the Island and around Vancouver.

A further study recommended dieselization of the 264.8 miles of the Calgary – Revelstoke transcontinental mainline. This single tracked section of the Laggan and Mountain Subdivisions featured grades exceeding 2.2% on the climbs to the passes in the Rocky and Selkirk Mountains in Southern British Columbia. A total of 26 A and 20 B passenger-service units was recommended for purchase along with 11 additional freight-service-only B units. Three GP7's were recommended as were six 1,000 horsepower S-4's for switching, plow trains and local freight and passenger service. GMDL received orders for nine A units and 25 B units, MLW delivered ten A units while CLC delivered seven A and six B units. All road units were geared for 65 mph and had dynamic brake equipment in deference to the steeply graded route. A Montreal - Vancouver test run of two FA-2's and two FB-1's in 1951 demonstrated not only the feasibility of diesel-electric operation in the mountains but pointed to the next phase of dieselization by train run that was adopted in 1953.

The final study adopted prior to the move to dieselization by train run and those leading to the final retirement of steam involved the Kootenay – Kettle Valley lines in Southern British Columbia and beyond to Medicine Hat, Alberta. In this instance adverse weather conditions in isolated, mountainous territory prevailed along with heavy mineral traffic on the lines to Kimberley and Tadanac near Cranbrook and Nelson. To handle the diversity of services including the through Medicine Hat – Vancouver passenger trains, the study recommended eight A and four B units equipped for passenger service with 18 A and four B units for freight service. Fourteen GP7's were recommended for local services with ten 1000 hp and eight 600 hp switchers. On delivery, MLW supplied two FPA-2 and two FPB-2 units for passenger service and ten FA-2's and six FB-2's; GMDL supplied the 14 GP7's, 10 FP7's and four F7B's (without boilers) while CLC provided six A and four B units. Six SW9's, four S-4's and five S-3's were also received. To simplify operating and maintenance issues upon implementation of the plan in 1953 the GM cab units and SW9's were assigned to Calgary, while eight A and six B passenger-equipped CLC units and the CPR's six other S-4's went to Nelson.

The impact of the dieselization by train run was strongly felt in Western Canada. The introduction of THE CANADIAN in 1955 and the conversion to diesel haulage of THE DOMINION withdrew 17 A and 12 B units from the Calgary – Revelstoke pool. This led to the purchase of the first GP9's, 8483 to 8521 of which the last 21 were equipped for dual-service. Subsequently two CLC passenger-equipped A-B sets (4104-05 and 4471-72) were acquired for assignment to Nelson to allow two pairs of dual-service MLW A-B (4082-83 and 4463-64) sets to be transferred to the Eastern Region. The ten lowest numbered GP9's replaced RS-3's 8426-8435 in Winnipeg-Edmonton-Calgary service. The RS-3's joined mates 8447-8461 in Montreal/Toronto – Winnipeg service while 8436-8446 replaced 11 Nelson-assigned GP7's reallocated to Revelstoke – Vancouver freights.

The first order for 21 RS-10 units (8462-8482) in 1954 was assigned to Vancouver – Montreal/Toronto secondary passenger trains. Seven of these boiler-equipped units were spares used predominantly in freight service. Yard units purchased at this time included the final eleven SW900's all for the Western Lines which also received seven of the fourteen S-3 units: 6530 to 6536. Seven SW900's replaced a like number of S-2's at Alyth Yard for reassignment on the Prairies.

Above ⊕ A thirty-two-page pamphlet from the mid 1960's offered career opportunities to new university graduates. (Bill Linley Collection)

In 1955, 24 GP9's were acquired for fast freights on the Prairies along with 6 CLC H16-44's for Lethbridge – North Portal freights and four for the passenger pool allowing four MLW cab units to be transferred to Montreal. In 1956 ten H16-44's (8601-8610) and 25 GP9's were delivered to Alyth for Western Lines fast freight service while 20 Train Masters joined the 8900 at Nelson. To balance motive power, six MLW cab units were sent east and 25 CLC's were re-assigned to Alyth.

H16-44's 8601-8610 left Alyth in 1957 to operate east of Nelson while 15 of the 20 similar units purchased that year replaced the last Nelson-assigned MLW units. Forty-seven of the 73 GP9's purchased in 1957 went to the Western Lines. In 1958 the purchase of MLW RS-18 units allowed 26 GP9's from the 1957 order to be transferred to the Western Lines. With the 23 newly purchased GP9's through freight service was completely dieselised on the Western Lines. Most of the first 25 of CPR's seventy-two SW1200RS units were delivered for service on Alberta branchlines and wayfreights.

In 1959, a further 15 GP9 units were purchased with the final dozen assigned to Winnipeg for Toronto – Calgary through service bumping eight older RS-10 and six FB-2 models from Chapleau to St. Luc in Montreal. Together with other measures, the advent of run-through power in the summer of 1959, notably on Toronto – Calgary trains, increased the utilization of units to the degree that complete dieselization was achieved in the spring of 1960 without additional road-unit purchases. Only eight new SW1200RS units were assigned to Winnipeg for secondary services in southern Manitoba and Saskatchewan.

Increasing traffic volumes and the aging of first generation units led to the purchase of additional four-axle power from GMDL in the form of two GP30's and 24 GP35's of which the first dozen GP35's were entirely new units. Similarly, 51 C-424's were purchased from MLW although all of these units had trade-in credits. Many of these new four motor units ran in Montreal/Toronto – Calgary fast freight service. Beginning in 1966, second generation SD40's arrived in orders for 32 and 33 units for service in the Western Mountains allowing the shifting of many FP7's, GP9's and CLC's away from the Calgary – Vancouver mainline. The era of tuscan and grey drew to a close in 1968 with the purchase of eight C-630M's from MLW.

Let's enjoy these colorful years on Canadian Pacific's Western Lines.

Assignment of Diesel Units & RDC's - Prairie & Pacific Regions - March 1, 1968

Location	Units Assigned
Fort William	6512-13/81/95
	6607-08
	7018/48-49/51/81-83,7101
	B-102-03
Kenora	6556/65
Winnipeg	4029/31,34-40
	4441-43
	6502-04/55/58-59/62-64/67-68/70/76-77/83/94/96-99
	6604-06/09
	7035/54-55/84-85/7102-05
	8104-11/19-22/25-29/65/68-71
	8409-12/14-19/21-24
	8483-8506/8530-46/8614-19/8691-8708/8801-09
	8911/13/18
Weston	12/21
Brandon	6554/57
Regina	6510/11/21
	7019
Moose Jaw	6531-32/34/82
	7037/50
Saskatoon	6522/33
	7036/53
	8013-18
	8112-18
Swift Current	6530/53
Medicine Hat	6719/20
Alyth	1900/1/3-5/7-8
	4030/33/61-63
	4424/27/31-33/35/37-40/44-48/59-62
	5500-64
	6516/17/19-20/35/36/78-9/6600/10/11
	6712-18
	8100-03
	8507-19/8611-13/20-90/8810-23/25-39
	9055-56; 9195-99
Edmonton	6710-11
Nelson	4052-57/64-65/76/77-81/4104-05
	4440-58/71-72
	7110/15
	8548-56/8601-10/8709-28
	8900/04/05
Penticton	7111/12
Coquitlam	7116/18
Vancouver	6518/22/72-74
	7065-75
	7100/06/07/09/14/17
	8005/6/9/12
	8903/9/17
Victoria	8000-4/7-8/10-11; 9023

Other units were also assigned as follows:

Ignace	6571
Dryden	6566
Portage La Prairie	11
Minnedosa	6580
Broadview	6569
Estevan	6505
Yorkton	10
Prince Albert	16
Revelstoke	7113
Kelowna	6575

Additions To Volume 1

Kentville	add 8140
North Bay	delete 6585; add 6592
Windsor	delete 6586
Toronto	delete 8111/12/18; add 6525/52;7029/46/57/93
Sudbury	delete 8160; add 7108
St. Luc	add 9100, 9194; add 7034/87
Sherbrooke	add 7015
Trois Rivieres	add 7042/45/62
Montreal (Glen)	add 6507/8/23/29/7012-14/30/41/56/58/76/79/80/86/88/90/95
Montreal (Glen)	transfer RDC's from St. Luc

(Bruce Chapman, Doug Hately collection)

CPR Roster January 1, 1949 to December 31, 1968

Numbers	Class	Model/Type	Builder	Date Built	Remarks
10-23	HS-5a-d	44-ton D-T-C	CLC	1957-60	
29,30,136,144	A1e, A2m,q	4-4-0	CPR, Rogers	1883-87	
417-1111, 2055-2119	D4g,D6a-d,D9c,D10b-e-g-h,k,E-5f-h	4-6-0	ALCO, CLC, CPR, MLW, North British, Saxony	1902-13	
1200-1301, 2200-2717	G5a-d,G1p,r-v,G2p-u,sx,ux G3a-j,G4a,b	4-6-2	CLC, CPR, MLW	1906-48	
1400-04, 16-18, 4028-41, 4061-63, 66-75	DPA-15a-d,DFA-15c-f	FP7	GMD	1950-3	Note 1
1405-15	DPA-17a	FP9	GMD	1954	
1800-02	DPA-22a	E8A	EMD	1949	
1900-07	DPB-17a	F9B	GMD	1954	
2800-64	H1a-e	4-6-4	MLW	1929-40	
2910-29	F1a	4-4-4	CLC	1937-38	
3000-04	F2a	4-4-4	MLW	1936	
3011, 63; 51	J3d;J5b	2-6-0	CPR; MLW	1888;1912	
3100-01	K1a	4-8-4	CPR	1928	
3360-3956	M3b,M4a-c-h,N2a-c,N4a-c	2-8-0	ALCO, Baldwin, CFDY, CLC, CPR, MLW	1902-21	
4000-27	DFA-15a,b	FA-1	ALCO, MLW	1949-50	
4042-51, 84-93	DFA-16a,e	FA-2	MLW	1951,53	
4052-57, 64-65	DFA-16b,c	CPA16-4	CLC	1952,51	
4076-81	DFA-16d	CFA16-4	CLC	1953	
4082-83, 94-98	DFA-16e,f	FPA-2	MLW	1953	
4104-05	DFA-16g	CPA16-4	CLC	1954	
4200-50	DRF-24a-c	C-424	MLW	1963-66	4200 ex 8300
4400-23	DFB-15a,b	FB-1	ALCO, MLW	1949-50	
4424-48, 59-62	DFA-15c,d	F7B	GMD	1951-52	4435-45 to 1909-19 & return
4449-54, 71-72	DFB-16a,d	CPB16-4	CLC	1952,54	
4455-58	DFB-16b	CFB16-4	CLC	1953	
4463-64	DFB-16c	FPB-2	MLW	1953	
4465-70	DFB-16c	FB-2	MLW	1953	
4500-07	DRF-30c	C-630M	MLW	1968	
5000-01	DRF-22a	GP30	GMD	1963	ex 8200-01
5002-25	DRF-25a,b	GP35	GMD	1964-65	ex 8202-13
5100-5473	P1d,e,n,P2a-h,j,k	2-8-2	CLC, CPR, MLW	1912-49	5200-64 rebuilt 36/37xx
5500-64	DRF-30a,b	SD40	GMD	1966-67	
5750-90	R2a,b,R3a-d	2-10-0	CPR	1909-19	
5800-14	S2a	2-10-2	CPR	1919-20	
5900-35	T1a-c	2-10-4	MLW	1929-49	
5997	T3a	0-6-4T	CPR	1912	
6152-6304	U3c-e	0-6-0	CPR	1905-13	
6500-6600, 6601-13, 14-23	DS-6a-h,j-k,m	S-3,S-10,S-11	MLW	1951-59	
6700-09, 10-20	DS-8a,b,DS-9a	SW8,SW900	GMD	1950-55	
6809-6968	P1d,e,n,P2a-h,j,k	2-8-2	Baldwin, CLC, CPR, MLW	1898-1931	
6950-6952	W1a	0-8-0	CPR	1914	
7010-64, 76-98; 7099-7118	DS-10a-e,h,j,k,m,n	0-10-0	ALCO, MLW	1943-1953	
7065-75	DS-10g	S-2;S-4	BLW/CLC	1948	
7400-05	DS-12a	DS4-4-1000	MLW	1953	
8000-12	DRS-10a	SW9	GMD	1948	
8013-46	DRS-10b-d	DRS4-4-1000	BLW/CLC	1959-60	
8100-71	DRS-12a-c	RS-23	MLW	1958-60	
8400-04, 8405-08	DRS-15a,b	SW1200RS	GMD	1949,50	
8409-25	DRS-15c,d	RS-2	ALCO, MLW	1952-53	
8426-61	DRS-16a,b	GP7	GMD	1954	
8462-82, 8557-8600, 8824	DRS-16c,e-g,k	RS-3	MLW	1954-57	8824 ex 4016 1st
8483-8546, 8611-8708, 8801-23, 25-39	DRS-17a-f	RS-10	MLW	1954-59	
8547-56, 8601-10, 8709-28	DRS-16d,h,j	GP9	GMD	1955-57	
8729-8800	DRS-18a,h	H16-44	CLC	1957-58	
8900-8920	DRS-24a-d	RS-18	MLW	1955-56	
8921		H24-66	FM/CLC, CLC	1957	
9020-24	DRS-24e	RSD-17	MLW	1953-56	
9049-72		RDC-3	Budd	1953-58	9049 ex DSS&A 500
9100-16, 94-99		RDC-1	Budd, CC&F	1951-58	9116 ex LV 41
9200,50-51		RDC-2	Budd, CC&F	1955-56	
B100-B103		RDC-4	Budd	1951-57	
		Slug	MLW		

Great Lakes Steamships

Above ● Passengers and onlookers await the traditional 3.15 p.m. departure of the CPR's *S.S. Assiniboia* on Saturday, August 15, 1964 just as they had done when this ship inaugurated service from the Railway's new Port McNicoll, Ontario harbor facility on another Saturday, May 4, 1912. To the left, one-of-a-kind Buffet Observation Parlor car 6630 (National Steel Car - Angus Shops, 1938) brings up the markers of Train 303, the connecting '*Steam Boat*' that had left Toronto at 12.01 p.m.
(Ted Wickson)

Above ● Constructed at Fairfield Shipbuilding and Engineering Company in Govan, Scotland, in 1907, the 3,880 gross ton *S.S. Assiniboia* was the flagship of the CPR's Great Lakes Steamships. The *S.S. Assiniboia* was converted from coal to oil firing with new water-tube boilers in 1953/54. With its Fairfield-built sister ship, the 3,856-ton *S.S. Keewatin*, Saturday departures were offered by the "Great White Twins" from both Port McNicoll and Fort William. The *Assiniboia* offered eastbound service on Tuesday mornings with a further westbound trip by the *Keewatin* on Wednesday. Just outside Port McNicoll on Saturday, July 20, 1957, the *Assiniboia* is up-bound on Georgian Bay and will deliver its passengers to Sault Ste. Marie the following morning and Fort William at 7.45 a.m. on Monday. *(John Mills)*

Left ⊕ The *Keewatin* is seen down-bound at the Canadian Soo Locks about noon on a Sunday in August 1953. The ship was retired in November 1966 and is on display in Saugatuck-Douglas, Michigan. The *Assiniboia* closed out the final two seasons of freight only service in November 1967. *(John MacIntosh, Bill Linley Collection)*

Bottom ⊕ The *Keewatin* enters the St. Mary's River on the same Sunday in August 1953 and is about to meet its up-bound running mate, the *Assiniboia*. The Algoma Central Railway's coal transfer bridge is the on port (left) side of the *Keewatin*. *(John MacIntosh, Ross McLeod Collection)*

Below ⊕ On arrival at dockside, passengers' baggage was transferred to a waiting, all-reserved-seat Fort William to Winnipeg coach that would be cut into Train 1, THE CANADIAN, prior to its 1.15 p.m. departure. CPR's last of thirty 1955 Budd-built coaches is seen from the *Assiniboia* at dockside in Fort William on Monday, July 30, 1962. The eastbound connection was made with THE DOMINION providing the necessary early morning arrival in Fort William. *(Doug Wingfield)*

Above ⊕ A 1964 brochure for the Great Lakes Services on the 'Inland Sea' offered up to 260 passengers the "thrills of an ocean voyage with the ceaseless activity of one of the world's busiest blue-water highways." At the time, all-inclusive return cruises were available for $100.

(Gerry Gaugl Collection)

PRAIRIE REGION
FORT WILLIAM DIVISION

Kaministiquia Sub

Above ⊕ DS-10h S-2 7083 drifts by the station opened in Port Arthur, Ontario in 1910 on the morning of Friday, September 27, 1968. The 1000 horsepower Montreal Locomotive Works unit was built in January 1949 by the Alco affiliate as the eighth of a 20-unit order for the first production switchers manufactured in Canada. *(Bill Linley)*

Below ⊕ In 1930-31, the Canadian Locomotive Company of Kingston, Ontario built the ten engines of class V5a, CPR's largest, newest and most powerful switchers with 22.5x32" cylinders, 58" drivers and 59,400 pounds of tractive effort. Designed and assigned to major terminals to handle increasingly heavy equipment, 6603, 6607 and 6608 were assigned to Fort William in 1952. 6608 is shown at Port Arthur in 1956.
(David Page)

Above ⊕ The Railway's Research Department completed a study in 1957 that called for complete dieselization by 1960, one part of which was a recommendation to acquire Branch Line Units of 1000 to 1200 horsepower to complement the 1600 to 1800 hp road switchers on which mainline freight operations were standardized. The BLU's could be used in many services like their steam counterparts, the D10 class 4-6-0's, and, in pairs could provide more starting tractive effort and horsepower than a single road switcher. Seen switching below the Pacific Avenue overpass on the east side of Fort William in April 1972, 8105 and 8107 were delivered in the early summer of 1958 as part of class DRS-12a, the first order for Branch Line Units: 31 London-built General Motors Diesel Ltd. SW1200RS's with Flexicoil trucks. *(George Rhine)*

Above ⊕ Double-headed Mikados, P2b 5324 (MLW 2-1921) and Kenora-assigned P2j 5443 (MLW 6-1944) depart Fort William circa 1957. The 5324, re-assigned to the Kaministiquia Freight pool from Kamloops, British Columbia between 1953 and 1955, will most likely be removed at the summit of Raith Hill some 60 miles to the west. *(David Page)*

Above ⊕ FP7 1426, class DPA-15c and F7B 1916 class DPB-15b await the 1.15 p.m. departure of Montreal – Vancouver Train 1, THE CANADIAN, at Fort William in December 1961. The previous evening, Toronto – Vancouver cars were added from Train 11 at Sudbury. A fifteen-minute stop provided an opportunity for through passengers to set their watches back one hour to Central Standard Time while the train was serviced and a new Fort William-based train crew boarded. Both of these 1952 built units had been renumbered and equipped with new 89 mph geared trucks in late 1954 from 4070 and in early 1955, 4442. This was done in preparation for the 54-unit high-speed passenger pool needed for the debut of THE CANADIAN in April 1955 and the concurrent dieselization of the accompanying DOMINION as well as Montreal – Toronto – Windsor Trains, 21 and 22. *(Keith Anderson)*

Left ⊕ On Saturday June 3, 1972, MLW-built FA-2 4088, class DFA-16e, leads a westbound returning empty 'grain box' to the Canadian Prairies from Fort William. Left-hand running is evident here as the original line of 1879 meanders along the banks of the Kaminisitiquia River while the newer, eastbound main of 1907 follows a straighter course in the background to the right of 4088's engineer. A siding appears in the foreground. Left-hand running began at a diamond mileage 2.4 in Fort William known as the "Criss-Cross" and continued to mileage 90.8 of the Keewatin Sub at Molson, Manitoba at a fly-over known as the "Hop-over." Built in September 1953 for service on the Kootenay and Kettle Valley Divisions in British Columbia, FA-2's 4087-4090 and FB-2's 4468-4469 were re-assigned to Chapleau, Ontario in the spring of 1957. *(Ken McCutcheon)*

Left ⊕ The first Canadian Pacific FA-2, (MLW 7-1951) 4042 leads an eastbound extra at Raith, mileage 45.5 on the Kaministiquia Sub in July 1969. Originally assigned to Schreiber on the North Shore of Lake Superior, this unit together with mate 4043 and FB-1's 4404 and 4405, led a transcontinental test freight in 1951 that was instrumental in the CPR's 1953 shift to dieselization by train run as compared to the previous, territorially-based program.

(Stan Smaill)

Left ⊕ The paralleling Trans-Canada Highway, Ontario Highway 17 is quiet on the afternoon of Sunday, September 8, 1968, but the CPR fields an eastbound at Argon, mileage 59.6 led by DRS-17d class unit GP9 8701. Part of the CPR's largest order for diesels, the 73 GP9's built by EMD's subsidiary, GMDL in London, Ontario, in October 1957, 8701 was originally assigned to the Eastern Region. By March 1, 1968 the 1750 hp unit was assigned to Winnipeg, Manitoba. *(Bill Linley)*

Ignace Sub

Above ⊕ Train 1 pauses at the division point of Ignace, Ontario to receive a fresh head-end crew. FP9 1413 (GMDL 5-1954) leads RS-10s 8577 and FP7 1400 at 5.30 p.m. on September 8, 1968. The FP9 was one of eleven – 1405 – 1415, class DPA-17a – purchased together with F9B units 1900 - 1907 for the 1955 debut of THE CANADIAN on the Montreal/Toronto – Vancouver run. The left-hand running is clearly visible at this station that fronts on the original, (now) westbound main line of 1880. *(Bill Linley)*

Right ⊕ Romance was featured in this 1963 equipment brochure. *(Gerry Gaugl Collection)*

Below ⊕ Once THE CANADIAN departed, FA-2 4090 with RS-10 8476 and FB-2 4468 arrived from the east with a drag freight and proceeded to the modest servicing facilities. S-3 6500 idles alongside the last remnants of the roundhouse southwest of the station at Ignace. The 6500 (MLW, 4-1951) is the first of 124, 660 horsepower MLW switchers purchased for use throughout the system, most notably in outlying terminals where their low horsepower was adequate for the assigned duties. The lack of a turbocharger on the 6-cylinder Alco 539 engine made for easier and less costly maintenance. *(Bill Linley)*

Keewatin Sub

Above ⊕ Canada's newest GP35, CPR 5025, class DRF-25c pulls up to the west end of the yard in Kenora, Ontario in June 1969. This unit and the 5024 were built by GMDL in January 1966 following extensive wreck damage to FP7 1401 and F9B 1906 on the eastbound CANADIAN near Schreiber, Ontario on Saturday, April 17, 1965. *(Stan Smaill)*

Below ⊕ Condensed Timetable 1949. *(Gerry Gaugl Collection)*

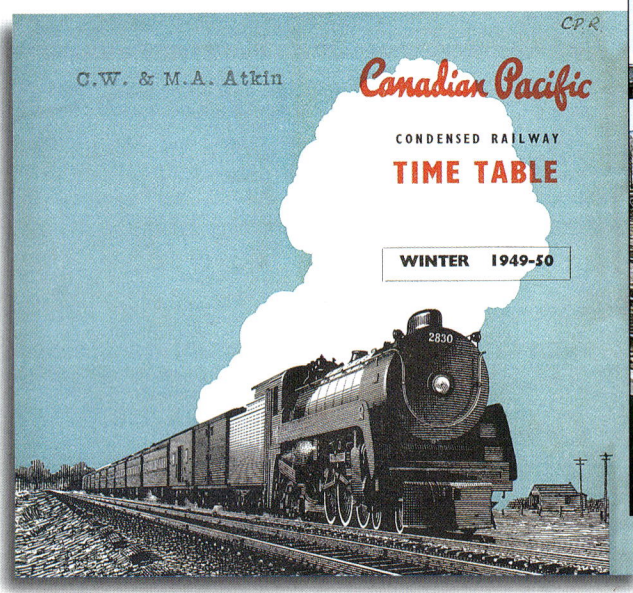

Above ⊕ The 1957 dieselization program featured the purchase of thirty-nine 660 hp MLW S-3's with 29 for the Western Lines including 6565, class DS-6h, seen switching opposite the Kenora passenger station in May 1967. *(Carl Gay)*

Above ⊕ Fort William to Winnipeg Train 53 pauses at Kenora, Ontario at 3.05 p.m. on Monday, July 22, 1957. Train 53 operated a tri-weekly, seasonal service, with limited stops on Mondays only, to provide a connection from the CPR's Great Lakes Steamships. Fort William-assigned H1d Royal Hudson 2854, with 75" drivers, 22x30" cylinders, 275 psi boilers and 45,300 lbs of tractive effort was built by MLW in April 1938. A trailing-truck booster provided another 12,000 lbs of tractive effort on starting a train. The H1d's, 2850 to 2859, were a subclass of the railway's 65 4-6-4's, all built by MLW including 45 streamlined versions that began to arrive in September 1937. The Royal designation was accorded following the tour of Their Majesties, King George VI and Queen Elizabeth in May 1939 when 2850 hauled the Royal Train without change from Quebec City 3,224 miles to Vancouver, BC. *(John Mills)*

Right ⊕ St. Luc-assigned class DRS-16a RS-3 8436 (MLW 4-1954) leads an FB-1 on a westbound freight between Kenora and Keewatin in October 1967. Note that this train is running on the right, "A.C.O.T.," against the current of traffic. The CPR's first order for RS-3's included 21 units of which the final eleven, 8436-8446 were initially assigned to relieve a like number of GP7's from the Kootenay and Kettle Valley Divisions in British Columbia. *(Carl Gay)*

Below ⊕ Class DRF-25a GP35 5008 leads an eastbound with a C-424 and a GP9 past the substantial Lake of the Woods Milling Company's flourmill in Keewatin, Ontario in April 1967. Benefiting from in-transit shipping rates, production began in 1888 and at peak capacity 62,000 bushels of wheat, roughly 45 carloads, were used to produce 10,000 bushels of flour daily – the largest such mill in the British Commonwealth. *Five Roses Flour* was their predominant brand. Fire claimed the mill in 1967. *(Carl Gay)*

Above ⊕ Extra 4047 East heels to the curve at Ingolf, Ontario, mileage 31.3 of the Keewatin Sub and just east of the Ontario – Manitoba border in July 1969. The trailing RS-2 8407 was one of four RS-2's in class DRS-15b assigned to Chapleau, Ontario when new from MLW in April 1950 for wayfreight service between Cartier and White River. *(Stan Smaill)*

Right ⊕ At Rennie, Manitoba, class DRS-24d H24-66 Train Master 8915 (CLC 9 -1956) leads a westbound string of empty boxcars just west of the Ontario border on Saturday, August 13, 1960. CPR purchased 20 of these units in 1956 following the purchase of the 8900 in 1955. The Canadian Locomotive Company units built to Fairbanks-Morse designs were intended to afford unit reduction in mainline service west of Calgary but they proved mechanically troublesome in service and were often stored. Fourteen units had been retired by early 1969. *(Bob Sandusky)*

Lac Du Bonnet Sub

Above ⊕ Seen around noon on a July day in 1959, tri-weekly mixed Train 502 from Winnipeg had left the Keewatin Sub at Whittier and traversed the 64.5 miles of the Lac du Bonnet Sub via Beausejour. This routing followed the original mainline of 1879 that had been bypassed by the Molson cut-off of 1907 as far as the second junction with the Keewatin Sub at Molson, mileage 43.6. The Lac du Bonnet Sub beyond Molson opened in 1907. The consist includes an auxiliary tender, a Hart gondola of ballast for the road master, a "mini" grain box and a combine of the 3300-3309 series. D10g class Tenwheeler, 926, (Angus 8-1911) was equipped with 63" drivers, 21x28" cylinders, and a 200 psi boiler producing 33,400 pounds of tractive effort. Representing the other 501 members of its class, roughly 17% of all CPR steam engines, 926 is preserved in the Canada Science and Technology Museum in Ottawa. *(Omer Lavallee, R. S. Ritchie Collection)*

Emerson Sub

Above ⊕ SW1200RS 8164 (GMDL 9-1960) switches at Emerson, Manitoba, on the border with North Dakota in May 1965. When new, CPR's final eight units of this type – 8164 - 8171 – were assigned to Winnipeg for wayfreight service in Manitoba and southeastern Saskatchewan. Constructed by the Federal Government and transferred to the CPR in 1881, the line to Emerson opened in 1879 and provided a connection with the St. Paul, Minneapolis and Manitoba Railroad, a Great Northern predecessor. Connections were established with the Northern Pacific in 1888, the Canadian Northern (CNR) in 1901 and the CPR controlled Soo Line in 1904. *(John Whitmore)*

Above ⊕ S-10 model switcher 6605, a cosmetic replacement for the S-3, (Class DS-6j, MLW 1-1958) is wying the Soo Line's St. Paul – Winnipeg consist, along with other equipment including the pictured 100 series CPR coach, at Mission Street in St. Boniface in August 1964. As a remnant of the discontinued Soo-Dominion via Portal, North Dakota, in the summer of 1964, The Winnipeger lifted a diner en route at Thief River Falls, Minnesota that joined a leased NYC *Valley* series 10-6 sleeper from St. Paul for the run to Vancouver on The Dominion. Whittier, just to the north beyond the overhead crossing of CNR's Redditt Sub, was an interlocked junction of the Lac du Bonnet and Emerson branches where the connecting Transcona Lead crossed the Molson Cut-off on the Keewatin Sub to form a wye. *(John Whitmore)*

Winnipeg Beach Sub

Above ⊕ In the last days of steam on this subdivision, G5d 1290 (CLC 6-1948) nears Riverton, the north end of the sub, 81.9 miles north of Rugby. Monday - Wednesday - Friday mixed Train 537 was due in Riverton at 3.35 p.m. on Friday, September 4, 1959 having left Winnipeg at 9.30 a.m. The return trip, Train 538, was to depart Riverton at 8.45 a.m. on Saturday for a 1.00 p.m. arrival. *(Lorne Perry)*

Above ⊕ Turning around, Lorne caught a 1954 Angus Shops-built center-cupola steel van trailing Train 537. This line opened 22.9 miles to Selkirk in 1883 and reached Riverton in 1914. Riverton was a jumping off point for the supply of materials to isolated communities in northern Manitoba on Lake Winnipeg. Many cottagers were also carried to communities along the shore of Lake Winnipeg. For example, in the summer of 1955 daily summer seasonal Trains 111 and 115 provided morning and evening departures for the Lake. Midday Saturday-Sunday-Wednesday Train 113 turned back as Train 114 from Gimli, mileage 56.5. Saturday only Train 120 left Gimli at 10.00 p.m. to accommodate day excursionists. From April 27th of that year, Trains 117 and 118 introduced same day return Dayliner (RDC) service from Winnipeg to Riverton as well as to the Lac Du Bonnet line. *(Lorne Perry)*

WINNIPEG TERMINAL DIVISION

Right ⊕ RS-10s 8573 (MLW 5-1956) and Soo Line (Wisconsin Central) GP9 2552 (EMD 12-1954) stand at CPR's Winnipeg station awaiting the last southbound departure of the WINNIPEGER, Train 110 – 10, for St. Paul, Minnesota at 6.45 p.m. on Sunday, March 26, 1967. The trailing consist was SOO Line baggage 47, coach 1954, sleeper 1259, CPR coach 1459 and baggage 4740. The class DRS-16f RS-10s was added to return the five-man train crew as well as the regular baggage man, news butcher and the last two cars back to Winnipeg from Emerson. A SOO Line crew took over their southbound Train 10 at Emerson. This station, crafted in local Tyndall limestone in the Beaux-Arts style, was designed by the Montreal firm of Edward and William Maxwell and opened in May 1905. The RS-10 was a Canada only MLW model superseding the RS-3 by providing more space in the carbody for a steam generator and dynamic brakes.
(Don Heron, Doug Phillips Collection)

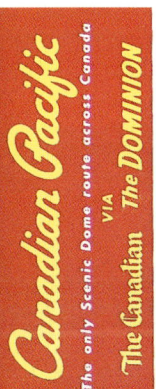

Left and Right ⊕ A ticket holder highlights the *Park* car on the world's longest scenic dome car service.
(Bill Linley Collection)

Below ⊕ Canada's only GP30's, CPR 8201 and 8200, team up to lead a westbound train past the Winnipeg Station on the afternoon of Friday, September 20, 1963. The pair was delivered by GMDL in London, Ontario on March 30, 1963 as wreck replacements for F9B 1902 and F7B 1910. Note the green flags indicating a following section of this scheduled train, possibly Montreal – Calgary Train 949. *(Keith Anderson)*

Above ◉ "Not a steamer in sight" was the photographer's notation on this view of mail and express Train 6 from the Salter Street Bridge as it nears the Winnipeg station behind a pair of RS-10's. The scheduled arrival time was 7.30 p.m. on this September evening in 1958. Toronto-bound Train 6 closely followed Train 8, the eastbound Montreal-bound DOMINION from Vancouver. At Sudbury, Ontario connections were provided on Trains 10 for Montreal and 4 for Toronto from Trains 6 and 8. Note FB-1 4413 and the two FB-2's on the ready tracks to the left of the image. At one time, the CPR's freight yards in Winnipeg were the largest in the British Empire. *(David Page)*

Right ◉ At 10.50 a.m. Tuesday, July 10, 1962, Train 7, THE DOMINION. departs Winnipeg for Vancouver behind CLC H16-44's 8725 and 8556 together with an FP7 trailing a long consist of head-end traffic, day coaches and perhaps some overflow traffic from the SOO-DOMINION. During the summer of 1962, the SOO-DOMINION ran ahead of THE DOMINION handling sleeping car and tour traffic from the U.S. and the East. Acquired along with six freight units in the summer of 1955, the DRS-16d class 8556 was the last of only four dual-service H16-44 units of Fairbanks Morse design. It was equipped for long hood forward operation while the class DRS-16j 8725 of the final order for these 1600 horsepower units in 1957 was set up to operate with the short hood leading. The steam generator was removed and 8556 was converted to short hood forward operation at Ogden Shops in Calgary, Alberta in November 1966. *(Peter Cox)*

Right ◉ A young Doug Cummings, latterly the publisher of *Extra 2200 South*, presses the cable release attached to his folding 616 camera to record a black-and-white view of G5b Pacific 1214 (MLW 9-1945) at the Winnipeg roundhouse on Monday, August 24, 1959. The 102 members of the G5 class of Pacifics were introduced in 1944 with the construction by the company's Angus Shops in Montreal of two samples of which the first, 1200, went to the Western Lines for evaluation. Designed to replace elderly Ten-wheelers and Pacifics of the D10, G1 and G2 classes, fifty of these modern engines were ordered from both MLW and then CLC between 1945 and 1948. Sixty-five of the 102 engines were assigned to the Western Lines at the end of 1952. 1214 had 70" drivers, 20x28" cylinders, a 250 psi boiler and 34,000 pounds of tractive effort. *(Keith Anderson)*

Above ◈ V3c 0-8-0 switcher 6907 (Angus 9-1913) pauses alongside Higgins Street on Thursday, April 23, 1959. The 10 V3c's, 6904 through 6913, were equipped with 52" drivers, 21x28" cylinders, a 200 psi boiler for a tractive effort of 40,400 pounds. 6907 was well traveled having been assigned to Trois Rivieres, Quebec on December 31, 1952 and was at St. Luc in October 1956.
(R. S. Ritchie)

Left ◈ The rear view of Train Master 8901 at Winnipeg in 1958 shows the full-width hood provided to the 8901 through 8904 to accommodate twin steam generators. This factory-installed option satisfied the need for four steam generator units for Medicine Hat – Vancouver Trains 67 and 68 operating through Nelson. These units released five 1600 horsepower boiler-equipped units for service based at Alyth diesel shop in Calgary. Breaking knuckles when mu'd in freight service cut short their assignment to the Southern British Columbia mainline. By December 1956, 8901 through 8903 were assigned to overnight Winnipeg – Moose Jaw locals 43 and 44. Train Masters were also used very briefly on Winnipeg – Edmonton Trains 51 and 52, the GREAT WEST. By 1960, most were assigned to Winnipeg – Fort William freight service.
(Bill Linley Collection)

Left ◈ Class R3b Decapod 5759 (Angus 9-1917) rests on Wednesday, September 22, 1956. The 2-10-0 was equipped with 58" drivers, 24x32" cylinders, a 200 psi boiler producing 54,000 pounds of tractive effort. Assigned to Nelson in 1952 the old-timer was working out its last miles in heavy switching service prior to scrapping in January 1958.
(William A. Swartz, Morning Sun Books Collection)

Above ⊕ En route from Winnipeg to Brandon on Saturday, August 29, 1959, Extra 2360 West passes Rugby Tower, built in 1947 with all electric controls, as part of a track improvement program at the west end of the Weston Yards, mileage 1.9. 2360 was built by CLC in November 1938 and was assigned to Moose Jaw, Saskatchewan in December 1952. A G3e class engine, it was one of the 15 engines of this subclass that was based on the 50 similar G3 engines built by MLW from 1923 through 1926. These dual-service engines were well suited to the Prairies and had a long reign at the headend of numerous freights. Specifications were 75" drivers, 23x30" cylinders, a 200 psi boiler and 42,500 pounds of tractive effort. *(Keith Anderson)*

Above ⊕ The engineer applies sand as an extra east accelerates through the interlocking with the La Riviere Sub at Rugby on Thursday, October 8, 1964. The interlocking at Rugby Junction also accessed the Winnipeg Beach and Arborg Subs to the north. 8839 of class DRS-17f (GMDL 8-1959) is a CPR one-of-a-kind late model GP9. Outshopped at GM's request with an upgraded 567D-1 prime mover for test purposes, it was essentially a GP18. A standard GM 567C was installed in the mid-1960s. *(Peter Cox)*

Right ⊕ This travel itinerary served passengers on THE CANADIAN and on Canadian Pacific Airlines in the early-1960's. *(Gerry Gaugl Collection)*

Above ⊕ On the double track of the 133.1-mile Carberry Subdivision, Train 2, THE CANADIAN, approaches Rugby behind a trio of RS-10s units led by 8565. The date is Wednesday, September 16, 1964 at about 10.30 a.m. The Carberry Sub was opened west from Winnipeg to Brandon in 1881 and double tracking was completed between 1911 and 1913. To the right of the train the smokestack in the distance marks the location of Weston Shops, CPR's major repair facility for the Prairie Region. *(Peter Cox)*

Above ⊕ Diesel-hydraulics 10 and 20 of classes HS-5a and d sit outside the east end of the locomotive repair facility at Weston Shops in July 1970. The shops opened in 1905 and repaired freight cars as well as performing major overhauls on both steam and diesel locomotives. First number 10 was one of fourteen similar CLC DTC (diesel torque converter) units built to Davenport designs at Kingston in March 1957. (CLC had acquired Davenport-Besler in 1955 including a stock of Porter locomotives). The units featured two 250 horsepower Caterpillar D337 6 cylinder in-line engines each driving a torque converter, a reverser and two-speed transmission with a drive shaft linked to an axle-mounted gearbox on the truck at the other end of the unit. The side rods powered the outer axles. The units were expected to weigh 44 tons in order to obviate the need for a fireman in shop and light duty yard service. 10 and 11 as delivered had overweight trucks and were subsequently rebuilt and delivered as 17 and 18, hence 10 as pictured was actually the third unit outshopped. *(Stan Smaill)*

Left ⊕ DRF-30b SD40 5557 (GMDL 4-1967) is coupled to Robot-1, car 4465 at Weston Shops on Canada Day, Monday, July 1, 1968. The 3000 hp SD40 was part of a follow-up order for 33 units following the purchase of an initial 32 units between July and December of 1966. Robot-1 was a former silk car from the 1920's later converted for baggage and express service. In 1967, it was equipped with CPR-developed remote control equipment to enable crewless operation of mid-train units in conjunction with conventional head-end power. The system was successfully tested at St. Luc on November 10, 1967 and became the basis for regular operation of remote-controlled units in unit train service, notably in the mountains west of Calgary.
(Stan Smaill)

Above ⊕ D10j 975 (MLW 9-1912) pulls through Woodman at mileage 5.7 with an eastbound extra on Tuesday, August 25, 1959. The 975 was assigned to Assiniboia, Saskatchewan at the end of 1952. Following service in Southern Saskatchewan, the 975 was assigned to the Manitoba District freight pool out of Winnipeg in November 1958 and to the Branch line pool in April 1959. Woodman was the east end of movement by signal indication on the two-track A.B.S. system that extended to Portage La Prairie. The line to the left is the 147 mile Glenboro Subdivision to Souris that opened in sections: 41.7 miles to Elm Creek in 1885, 52.9 miles to Glenboro in 1886, 27.3 miles to Nesbitt in 1891 and the final 18.8 miles in 1892. *(Jim Walder, John Riddell Collection)*

Below ⊕ On Friday, August 17, 1959, another eastbound extra, led by Brandon-assigned P1n class 2-8-2 5216, approaches Woodman. The light, modern Mikado featuring 22x28" cylinders, 63" drivers, and a 215 psi boiler producing 45,000 pounds of tractive effort was outshopped by Angus in November, 1947 as a rebuilding of 2-8-0 3715 (MLW 11-1912). Sixty-five of these engines were produced in an in-house rebuilding program that ran from November, 1946 through to the delivery of CPR's newest steam engine, 5264 in December, 1949. As dieselization progressed in 1959 serviceable steamers were concentrated in areas such as Winnipeg. 5216 had been based in Hardisty, Alberta at the end of 1952. The 5216 was a survivor having languished at Ogden from April 1957 through May 1958 before returning to service in Manitoba.
(Jim Walder, John Riddell Collection)

BRANDON DIVISION

Glenboro Sub

Above ⊕ DRS-17b GP9 8545 (GMDL 7-1955) is switching at Cypress River, mileage 91.9 from Woodman with the eastbound tri-weekly wayfreight on Thursday, May 11, 1972. This line began construction in 1881 under the charter of the Manitoba Southwestern Colonization Railway and was completed through to Regina in 1904. Although through passenger Trains 55 and 56, later 39 and 40, ran from end-to-end until the fall of 1958, it was not used as a through freight line. *(Bill Hooper)*

GP7 8422 from the CPR's second and final order for GP7's was delivered in May 1953 as part of the dieselization of the Kootenay - Kettle Valley Regions. On Thursday, May 18, 1972, the 1500-horsepower unit rests on the Shop Track opposite the 1912 station and former dispatching office at Souris. Considerable grain volumes moved from southeastern Saskatchewan over the Kisbey and Arcola Subdivisions east of Weyburn to Schwitzer, 5.4 miles west of Souris on the Estevan Sub. This traffic joined coal tonnage from Bienfait near Estevan and was forwarded beyond Souris to the main line at Brandon via the Broadview Sub junction at Kemnay. *(Bill Hooper)*

Carberry Sub

Above ⊕ G3d Pacific 2343 is eastbound at Portage La Prairie on Monday, August 17, 1959. Built by MLW in September, 1926 the dual-service 4-6-2 is equipped with a 250 psi boiler, 75" drivers, 23x30" cylinders and produced a tractive effort of 45,000 lbs. The engine was assigned to Winnipeg at the close of 1952 and was scrapped in September 1964. Brandon-assigned sister 2341 is preserved at Exporail in Saint-Constant, Quebec.

(Jim Walder, John Riddell Collection)

Above ⊕ In 1960, the CPR placed an order for five D-T-C's, including 21, which turned out to be CLC's final domestic order from a Canadian railway. 21 is returning to the yard in Portage La Prairie from the Campbell's Soup plant with a short string of canned soup-filled insulated boxcars. The Campbell's plant opened in 1960 to serve Western Canadian needs. The photographer noted that the crew provided him with several cans of soup courtesy of the loading dock employees. The cans, however, were unlabelled, so as his westward journey continued, dinner commenced with the opening of yet another can of "mystery soup" which was always a surprise, but never a disappointment. *(Ken Goslett)*

Broadview Sub

Above ⊕ CPR operator Stan Smaill was deadheading west to Calgary for an appointment with the Steel Gang in June 1967. Stan took this photograph of Train 5, the Expo Limited, at 2.10 p.m. while stretching his legs during the 15-minute station stop in Brandon. This train was a single season reincarnation of The Dominion as part of Canadian Pacific's contribution to Canada's Centennial year. The CPR also operated a corporate pavilion at the *Man and His World* World's Fair in Montreal. Lead unit 4094 is one of CPR's final five FPA-2's delivered by MLW in November 1953 for Toronto – Windsor fast-freight service. The distinctive spires of St. Mary's Ukrainian Catholic Church, completed in 1941 to mark the 50th anniversary of the arrival of the first Ukrainians in Canada, are to the left of the train at 10th Street and Assiniboine Avenue. *(Stan Smaill)*

Right ⊕ The *Faresaver Plan* was a response to CN's *Red, White and Blue* incentive fares of the early 1960's and offered a Montreal – Vancouver roomette in the low season for $78.45 or with nine meals included for $94.50.

(Bill Linley Collection)

Below ⊕ Montreal – Vancouver Train 7, The Dominion, is about to depart from an unscheduled stop at Kemnay on Saturday, June 18, 1960 having just set off a bad order car opposite the CO-OP elevator. Like 4094, 1402 was purchased in 1953 as one of five FP7's for Toronto – Windsor fast freights. Originally geared for a non-standard 77 mph to enhance compatibility with the 75 mph gearing of the FPA-2's, this was deemed unsuccessful and they were soon regeared to 89 mph and renumbered from 4099 to 4103 to 1400 through 1404 for the debut of The Canadian.

(George M. Leilich)

Above ⊕ "West of Brandon" the slide caption reads as G3h 2451 (CLC 2-1945) handles a westbound dimensional flat loaded with a crane on Thursday, September 3, 1959. The G3h was yet another subclass of the G3 series of Pacifics of which the semi-streamlined versions ran from 2351 through 2472. MLW built the last ten in 1948 while CLC built the rest from 1938 through 1945.
(Robert Trennert)

Above ⊕ GP9 8677 (GMDL 7-1957) leads an eastbound Broadview Sub train at Virden, Manitoba, mileage 47.2 of the Brandon – Broadview, Saskatchewan mainline. Rails reached Virden on the through route to the Pacific Coast in early 1882. Grain and other traffic mushroomed with the on-going settlement of the West and double tracking reached Virden from Winnipeg by 1914. With the installation of a second track on the Molson Cutoff east of Winnipeg in 1927, double track was continuous over the 605.8 miles from Virden to Current River, the eastern boundary of CPR's Western Lines some 6.4 miles east of Fort William, Ontario. *(Ken McCutcheon)*

Above ⊕ G3g 4-6-2 2389 (CLC 5-1942) is westbound on Sunday evening, August 16, 1959. Vancouver, B.C. had been home to 2389 in 1952 followed by an assignment to Alyth and then to Saskatoon by May 1958. The scene is at Fleming, Saskatchewan, four miles west of the Manitoba border at mileage 77.7 of the 130.9 Broadview Sub. Until recently, Fleming was the site of the oldest (1895) grain elevator still standing in Western Canada. *(Jim Walder, John Riddell Collection)*

Above ⊕ SW1200RS 8164, class DRS-12c, (GMDL 9-1960) is slowing to spot the stock car at the west end of Wapella, mileage 102.4 on Monday, June 29, 1964. Note the semaphore signals on this stretch of ABS single track that extended from Virden 55.2 miles to Whitewood 14.4 miles east of Broadview. The CPR installed Union Switch & Signal model T2 upper-quadrant semaphores in this stretch of track over two years. Virden to Kirkella was completed in 1925 with the installation of 54 signals and Kirkella to Whitewood was completed in 1926. By the end of 1964 the semaphore signals disappeared when CPR completed the conversion of the Virden to Whitewood segment to centralized traffic control and eliminated the passing siding seen here. Wapella, birthplace of photographer Doug Phillips, had another siding on the north side of the mainline whose east switch began east of the west switch of the pictured siding. These lapped sidings were dubbed "poor man's double track" and were the site of many three way meets prior to the installation of CTC. *(Bob Geveart, Bill Linley Collection)*

Right ◉ GP9 8805 rests at the end of track at Miniota, mileage 71.6, on Tuesday, May 16, 1972 with the bi-weekly wayfreight from Brandon. Shortly, it will turn on the wye for the return trip. The Miniota Sub was part of a network of branches known as the North Branches that extended between the Mainline and the Winnipeg – Edmonton North Line. Rails were laid south and west of Minnedosa under the charters of the Manitoba and Saskatchewan Railway and the Great North West Central Railway and reached Miniota on the brow of the Assiniboine Valley in 1901. *(Bill Hooper)*

Miniota Sub

Below ◉ Returning to Brandon, 8805 is about to cross the Arrow River near mileage 63 of the Miniota Sub and has just ducked under the CNR Winnipeg – Vancouver mainline near their Quadra siding. The Grand Trunk Pacific, a CNR predecessor, completed their mainline in 1907. *(Bill Hooper)*

Neudorf Sub

Above ◉ Eastbound Neudorf – Virden Train 96 led by DRS-17e class GP9 8814 (GMDL 2-1958) nears the junction of the Neudorf Sub with main line at Virden in August 1970. The eastern section of the Neudorf Sub opened over the 36.4 miles to McAuley, Manitoba in 1913. The original line through McAuley had opened in 1904 as the Pheasant Hills Branch over the 16.8 miles from the mainline at Kirkella, Manitoba and extended northwest a further 89.8 miles to Neudorf, Saskatchewan where it connected with the Bulyea Sub. The Bulyea Sub opened in 1905 and continued 86.4 miles west to Bulyea where it connected 43.1 miles north of Regina with the Lanigan Sub. In the early days of steam, to avoid tonnage restrictions on the steeply graded Bredenbury Sub, grain drags from the branches around Lanigan would operate via a terminal at Strasbourg, mileage 50.5 on the Lanigan Sub and run via Neudorf and McAuley and then over the 16.8-mile McAuley Sub to terminate at Elkhorn, mileage 70.3 on the Broadview Sub, some 7.4 miles east of Kirkella. In later years, trains operated over the entire length of the Neudorf Sub en route to Brandon. The McAuley Sub was abandoned in 1962. *(Bill Hooper)*

Bredenbury Sub

Above ⊕ At Minnedosa, Manitoba on Thursday, May 11, 1972, a van is about to be exchanged for an outbound freight on the Minnedosa Sub to Portage La Prairie and beyond on the Carberry Sub to Winnipeg. Following the abolition of yard crews at this division point, 77.9 miles west of Portage La Prairie, a road crew used S-11 DS-6m switcher 6619 (MLW 7-1959) to make the exchange. The MLW-only S-11 was a redesign of the S-10 of 1958, (CP 6601-6613) which moved the radiator to the front of the unit, used a higher frame and better cab insulation. 6619 had formerly replaced steam on the Kingston & Pembroke line in Eastern Ontario and since 2005 has been displayed at the Barr Colony Heritage Museum in Lloydminster, Saskatchewan. *(Bill Hooper)*

Above ⊕ Winnipeg – Saskatoon Train 977, commonly called "The Hooks," because of the double sevens in its number, backs out of the yard and past the station to marshal its train prior to ascending the 1.6 % westbound grade leaving Minnedosa. It would encounter a ¾ mile stretch of 2% at mileage 1.9. Train 977 will have a 118.6-mile run over the Bredenbury Sub. DRS-15c class GP7 8410 leads an F7B on May 11, 1972. Built in March 1952, as the second of three similar units for wayfreight service as part of the dieselization of the Laggan and Mountain Subdivisions on the mainline west of Calgary, 8410 and 8411 were briefly equipped with steam generators for use on seasonal specials and ski trains. Minnedosa sits in a bowl and outbound steam-era trains were often assisted by R1 series 2-10-0's, the only such engines assigned to mainline freights on the Prairies. *(Bill Hooper)*

Estevan Sub

Right ⊕ Thursday-only mixed Train 551 is westbound at Hartney, mileage 32.3 at 10.30 a.m. on June 4, 1959. Just ahead is the interlocked diamond with the CNR's Hartney Subdivision, which had been opened east of Hartney in 1900 by the Manitoba Railway Company, a subsidiary of the Northern Pacific. Having left Souris at 9.50, Train 551 will traverse 50.4 miles of the Estevan Sub to Napinka where it will turn east on the Napinka Sub for 18.8 miles to Deloraine. Turning again to the southwest, it will follow the 37.2 miles of the Lyleton Sub to the village of that name for a scheduled 2.55 p.m. arrival. G5b 4-6-2 1213 (MLW 9-1945) will depart at 8.20 a.m. the following day with Train 532 to Deloraine, thence via the Napinka Sub 21.1 miles to Boissevain where it will turn to the north and west over the 35.5 miles of the Boissevain Sub to a crossing of the Estevan Sub at Lauder, just 41.6 miles from Souris. At 2.50 p.m. it will depart over the Alida Sub to Alida, Saskatchewan, 53.9 miles to the west. Finally, at 7.30 a.m. on Saturday as Train 552, it will depart Alida for a 10.55 arrival in Lauder and thence directly back to Souris on the Estevan Sub for a scheduled arrival at 12.15 p.m. *(R. S. Ritchie)*

Left ⊕ Train 86 is eastbound from Estevan to Souris along the north side of the Souris River nearing Oxbow, Saskatchewan, mileage 114.7 of the Estevan Subdivision on a June morning in 1972. GP9's 8803 and 8485 provide the power. *(Ken McCutcheon)*

Below ⊕ Eastbound Train 86 passes the coal staging yard at Bienfait, mileage 147.6 of the 156.1-mile Estevan Sub in June 1972. A wye connection is made here with the Manitoba and Saskatchewan Coal Company's railway and a source of much coal traffic destined to the Lakehead over the Estevan Sub. CPR rails reached Estevan from Brandon in 1892. *(Ken McCutcheon)*

REGINA DIVISION

Indian Head Sub

Above ⊕ THE DOMINION, Montreal – Vancouver Train 7, is serviced at the Division Point of Broadview, Saskatchewan, at 5.00 p.m. Mountain Standard Time on Monday, September 17, 1951. Broadview marks the beginning of the Regina Division and the point where clocks were set back one hour from Central Standard Time for westbound trains. H1c Hudson 2845 (MLW 11-1937) was an oil burner assigned to Winnipeg at the close of 1952 and will depart with a new crew. *(R. S. Ritchie)*

Above ⊕ Regina assigned G3h Pacific 2445 (CLC 1-1945) rests by a standpipe at the Broadview roundhouse on Sunday, August 16, 1959. The engine wears a simplified paint scheme devoid of outlining around the tender and along the running board as shown in the accompanying shot of 2449. A few engines wore this informal paint scheme as applied to 2449 at Weston Shops in Winnipeg in the closing months of steam operation on the Western Lines. The graphited smokebox was a standard feature unique to Western Lines engines. *(Jim Walder, John Riddell Collection)*

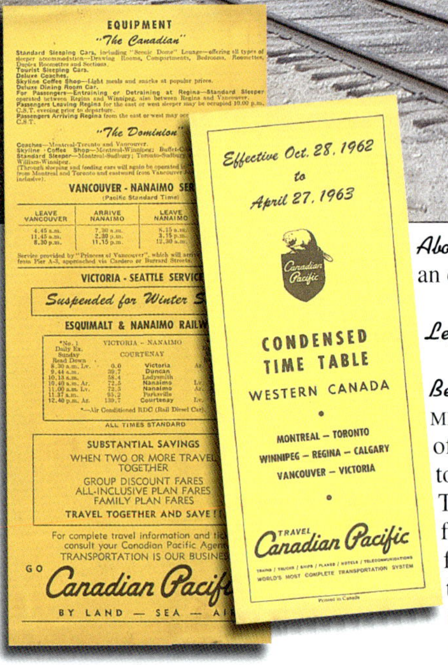

Above ⊕ Conventionally painted G3h, 2449, assigned to Moose Jaw, is about to depart Broadview with an eastbound extra freight in July 1952. *(William J. McChesney, Morning Sun Books Collection)*

Left ⊕ Condensed timetable for Western Canada. *(Gerry Gaugl Collection)*

Below ⊕ V4a class 0-8-0 6937 (MLW 9-1908 as M4h 2-8-0 3538), switches Train 8, the eastbound DOMINION, in Regina at 9.10 a.m. on Thursday, September 1, 1959. Rails reached Regina at mileage 93.5 of the Indian Head Sub in 1882. The set-off from Vancouver would include an "F" series 13 section tourist sleeper and an 8 section, one drawing room, two compartment "R" series heavyweight sleeper. The thirty engines of the V4a class, 6920 – 6949, were converted at Angus Shops in 1928 and 1929 from M4g & M4h Consolidations. The reduction to 52" drivers from the original 58" was the primary feature of the rebuilding which resulted in a switcher carrying 180 psi boiler, 22.5x28" cylinders with tractive effort increased by 4,300 pounds to 41,700 pounds. The gain in pulling power was substantial enough that there were many informal conversions of M4's to 0-8-0's through the simple expedient of removing the pony truck until a visit from company officials was expected. *(Keith Anderson)*

Above ⊕ In June 1907, the Baldwin Locomotive Company of Philadelphia, Pennsylvania, completed and shipped 2-8-0 number 1722 to the CPR. The locomotive was renumbered as 3522 in September 1912. In 1930, it was assigned to Newport, Vermont on the New England lines. Displaced by dieselization in the early 1950's, the engine was assigned to Regina by the end of 1952. Affectionately known as "Thirty-five Tooty-two," the switcher did not receive the typically CPR high-mounted switcher headlight. Equipped with 22.5x28" cylinders, 58" drivers, a 180 psi boiler, the M4g class engine generated 37,400 pounds of tractive effort. The 3522 was sold for further use by the Manitoba and Saskatchewan Coal Company at Bienfait, Saskatchewan, near Estevan in October 1956 where it ran until 1965. In 1968 it was placed on display in Bienfait. Bill McChesney pictured the engine from an eastbound train at Regina in July 1952. *(Morning Sun Books Collection)*

Right ⊕ Brandon assigned Jubilee 4-4-4 2911 (CLC 11-1937) rests at the 'Shops' in Regina, Saskatchewan on Wednesday, October 17, 1956. Tractive effort of 25,900 lbs was generated from the 300-psi boiler transmitting steam to 16.5 x 28" cylinders powering 75" drivers. The second of twenty similar class F1a engines ordered from Canadian Locomotive Co. in 1937, it was designed for high-speed intercity passenger services hauling the new, lightweight 2100 series coaches. These trains never materialized and fifteen of the engines became the assigned power for many secondary passenger services across the Prairies. Although hand-fired, their relatively light duties and modern features made them easy to fire and run. The name Jubilee was derived from the commemoration of the fiftieth anniversary of Montreal – Vancouver through passenger service when the wheel arrangement was introduced to the CPR with the arrival from MLW of the F2a class 80"-drivered 3000 series in 1936. Note the absence of the usual tuscan red panels on the tender and running boards.
(William A. Swartz, M.D. McCarter Collection)

Right Center ⊕ On Thursday, October 18, 1956, Bill Swartz found another passenger service engine, G2s class Pacific 2595 on the ready tracks adjoining the 12-stall roundhouse in Regina. This hand-fired engine was built at Angus in June 1910 as the second 1165 with 70" drivers, 21x28" cylinders and a 200 psi boiler with a tractive effort of 30,000 lbs. It was rebuilt in November 1930 with larger 22.5X28" cylinders yielding a tractive effort of 34,500 pounds. The light weight of this 120-ton engine would enable its use on branchlines throughout Saskatchewan for a further three years thereby outlasting many of its newer and heavier brethren. *(William A. Swartz, M.D. McCarter Collection)*

Right ⊕ Circa 1955, Train 6 out of Vancouver for Toronto led by Royal Hudson 2843 passes Pasqua, mileage 128.3, 6.8 miles east of Moose Jaw. The junction switch begins the Portal Sub, the direct, 628-mile route to St. Paul, Minnesota via the Soo Line connection at Portal, North Dakota. Train 6 nick-named "THE ADVANCE DOMINION" ran ahead of THE DOMINION, Train 8, making more stops and handling Train 8's overflow traffic, particularly mail and express, during the summer period. *(Ron Bearman)*

Lanigan Sub

Above ⊕ Train 92 arrives in Regina from Colonsay on Tuesday afternoon, August 3, 1965. Note the "station water car" used to deliver water to wayside stations and section-houses. The northwestern end of the 108.5 miles Colonsay Sub was at Colonsay, a junction with the Wynyard – Saskatoon Sutherland Sub. The final leg of the run from Euston, junction with the Lanigan Sub, was over 24.3 miles of the Lanigan Sub into Regina. The Colonsay Sub opened in 1911 as the CPR's replacement for a Regina – Saskatoon line operated for the Qu'appelle, Long Lake and Saskatchewan Railroad and Steamboat Company. The termination of this arrangement in 1906 transferred this line to the Canadian Northern (CNR). *(John Rushton)*

Above ⊕ The Lanigan Sub extends 104.4 miles north from Regina to a connection at Lanigan with the Sutherland Sub on the 'Prairie North Line' 75.8 miles east of Saskatoon. Until October 25, 1958, this was the route of overnight passenger Trains 203/204 to and from Prince Albert with a connection to Trains 205/206 for Saskatoon at Lanigan. Train 96's days of handling express are numbered on August 3, 1965 as SW1200RS 8127 leads the southbound at Drake, 6.9 miles out of its home terminal at Lanigan en route to Regina. At Bulyea, the local met westbound Train 97 out of Neudorf at the east end, mileage 86.4, of the Bulyea Sub. The two trains were consolidated and ran together for the last 43.1 miles into Regina. During construction, rail laying progressed along the Neudorf Sub in 1905 through Bulyea to Strasbourg and reached Lanigan in 1907. The connection from Bulyea via Euston to Regina was completed in 1911. *(John Rushton)*

Portal Sub

Above ⊕ The Portal Sub runs southeasterly from the mainline junction with the Indian Head Sub 160.6 miles to North Portal on the Saskatchewan – North Dakota border. It was opened in 1893 as an extension of the CPR-controlled Soo Line to provide a joint route from the Twin Cities to the Pacific Northwest in competition with the Great Northern and the Northern Pacific. At McTaggart, mileage 75.9, GP7 8416 is paired with GP9 8823 on a ballast-spreading work train on Tuesday, June 7, 1960. The McCabe Brothers Grain Co was headquartered in Winnipeg from 1915 until 1968 when the United Grain Growers purchased their more than 100 elevators. McCabe's subsidiary, the Victoria Elevator Company focused on south-central Saskatchewan. *(Bob Sandusky)*

Above ⊕ CPR H16-44 8554, class DRS-16d (CLC 6-1955) heads a westbound North Portal to Moose Jaw train at Weyburn, mileage 84.7. Weyburn was an important grain shipping point and a junction with the 61.8-mile Kisbey Sub that ran to the east to join the Regina – Souris – Winnipeg line at Stoughton. The 110.5-mile Assiniboia sub ran west to Assiniboia. This unit was one of the first order for H16-44's, 8547-8556 in 1955 of which the first six were for North Portal – Lethbridge freights while the final four were additions to the western pool of dual service units. The DRS-16d and DRS-16h series (8601-8610) were built for long hood first operation; however, between 1963 and 1967 all but 8554 and 8555 had the controls reversed for better visibility and reduced fume effects. The 8554 survived as part of the CPR's small collection of preserved diesel units based in Calgary. *(Bob Sandusky)*

Above ⊕ Train Master 8901 pauses at Weyburn with North Portal-bound local Train 204, the Soo-Dominion, at 10.55 a.m. on Sunday, May 22, 1960. The Soo Line would add an 8-1-2 sleeper at North Portal for the connecting run of their Train 14 to St. Paul. The local would be cut back to Moose Jaw – Estevan for the summer of 1960, the last year of seasonal operation of the Mountaineer, a through train from St. Paul to Moose Jaw with connections onward on The Dominion. The Soo-Dominion would replace the Mountaineer on this route for one final summer in 1961. On May 31, 1961 the last runs of Trains 13 and 204, the Portal Local on the Moose Jaw – North Portal route would bring an end to the need for the Train Masters in passenger service. The twin steam generators were removed and the short hood narrowed to the normal width. Subsequently, the controls were repositioned so that the short hood became the front.
(Bob Sandusky)

Right ⊕ Canadian Pacific money orders were available at stations and ticket offices across the country.
(Bill Linley Collection)

Below ⊕ DS-6a class S-3 6505 pauses in front of the station at Estevan, mileage 137.5 in October 1972. Originally assigned to Alyth Yard in Calgary, the unit was one of the initial order for six units in 1951 that were closely observed to ensure that the reduction in horsepower from the 1000 hp S-4 would not compromise yard operations. Estevan was the junction point for the Estevan Sub leading eastwards to Souris, as well as the grain-gathering Bromhead Sub to the west. The name Estevan was derived from a combination of the names of George Stephen and William C. Van Horne, the company's first and second presidents. The Estevan station opened in 1927. *(Stan Smaill)*

Above ⊕ Extra 8537 South ascends the grade at milepost 151 nearing Pinto en route out of the Souris River Valley heading for North Portal in November 1972. The trailing unit is leased from Precision National and is the highest numbered GP7 of twenty originally owned by the Quebec, North Shore & Labrador. Built at London in August 1952 as 123, it went to the Chicago & Northwestern as their 4342 in 1976. *(Ken McCutcheon)*

Bromhead Sub

Above ⊕ GP9 8837 is seen in October 1972 with a westbound extra on the Bromhead Sub. D10j 975 seen previously at Woodman, Manitoba had been assigned to Estevan to work the Neptune – Bromhead mixed in May 1958. The 54.1-mile Neptune Sub was opened west of Estevan in 1913 to Neptune. In 1927, the Bromhead Sub, a 26.2-mile branch from Southall, mileage 34.1, opened southwestwards to Lake Alma. In 1930, this branch was extended a further 28.7 miles to Minton. In 1961, the Southall to Tribune section was reduced to the Tribune Spur and the trackage beyond to Neptune was abandoned. At this time, the entire 79 miles from Estevan to Southall to Minton were renamed as the Bromhead Sub. *(Ken McCutcheon)*

MOOSE JAW DIVISION

Outlook Sub

Above ⊕ The grain is moving on Tuesday, September 10, 1968 as a southbound extra passes Marquis, mileage 22, behind GP9 8646. This DRS-17c class Geep was another of CPR's largest order for GP9s – 73 units, 8636 through 8708 – and arrived in February 1957. In 1904, Sir Charles Saunders working at the Dominion Experimental Farm in Ottawa developed *Marquis*, a strain of hard, spring wheat that had good milling qualities and matured seven to ten days earlier than other varieties. The rapid ripening encouraged northward settlement doubling the area under production. By 1920, more than 90% of the 17 million acres of wheat grown on the Canadian Prairies was of this variety. The village of Marquis was founded in 1910. *(Bill Linley)*

Left and Above ⊕ Extra 8646 South passes Tuxford, mileage 15.2 en route to Moose Jaw on September 10, 1968. In 1908, this 120.4-mile line to the northwest of Moose Jaw opened as far as Outlook on the banks of the South Saskatchewan River. Outlook was the eastern end of the Kerrobert Sub that extended a further 102.5 miles to Kerrobert. At Kerrobert, the Macklin Sub continued for 46.4 miles to the northwest to Macklin creating a through route from Edmonton to Moose Jaw. Macklin was almost at the mid-point between Saskatoon and Wetaskawin, (42 miles south of Edmonton, Alberta) on the 'Prairie North Line'. The brakeman in van 437192 receives a wave from a sectionman as he eyes the photographer. The van was one of 255 similar 34-foot 10 inch-long, steel-underframed cars rostered on January 1, 1956. *(Two photos, Bill Linley)*

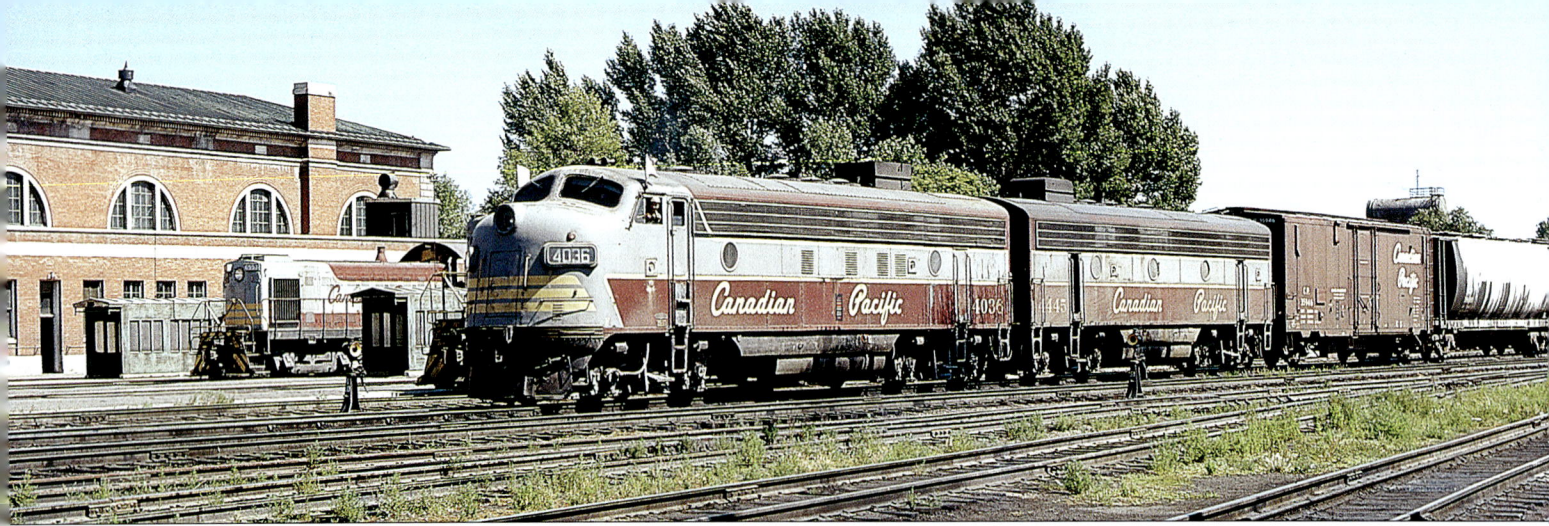

Above ⊕ A westbound extra behind FP7 4036 arrives at Moose Jaw on Tuesday, August 8, 1970. The FP7 was from the first Canadian order placed with General Motors Diesel Limited at its new plant in London. This subsidiary of GM's Electromotive Division of La Grange, Illinois went on to become the largest and most long-lived supplier of locomotives to Canadian railways. CPR's 10-unit order for FP7's was delivered in 1950 for the dieselization of the Schreiber Division main line in Northern Ontario. Assigned to the newly opened diesel shop in Chapleau, they shared road duties with 20 new MLW FA-1's and 10 FB-1's. Between March and May 1952, they returned to London for the installation of steam generators prior to being assigned to passenger service west of Calgary. CPR ordered no F7A's preferring the versatility of the FP7 that was shown again when the steam generator was removed from 4036 in September 1966. Trailing unit DFB-15d class F7B 4445 (GMDL 4-1952) was regeared (62:15 to 58:19) for 89 mph versus the freight train standard of 65 mph and renumbered 1919 for passenger service between the anticipated advent of THE CANADIAN in October 1954 and the expected discontinuance of THE DOMINION in November 1965. Moose Jaw assigned S-3 6553 waits in the background. *(Bill Linley Collection)*

Swift Current Sub

CANADIAN PACIFIC RAILWAY

PRAIRIE REGION - SASKATCHEWAN DISTRICT

TIME 82 TABLE

TAKING EFFECT AT 24.01 O'CLOCK SUNDAY, APRIL 26th, 1953

GOVERNED BY MOUNTAIN STANDARD TIME

FOR THE INFORMATION AND GUIDANCE OF EMPLOYEES ONLY

E. S. McCRACKEN, General Manager — C. E. LISTER, General Superintendent

Right ⊕ Saskatchewan District Employees Timetable, April 26, 1953. *(Bill Linley Collection)*

Below ⊕ Although originally assigned to Calgary, Alco S-2 switcher 7037 was long-assigned to Moose Jaw. It was the final unit of the 1945 order for 13 S-2's and was outshopped in Schenectady, New York in August. Here, on Tuesday, September 10, 1968, it pulls by the divisional office wing of the station that opened in 1922 as one of the last major new stations opened by the Railway. The clock on the Italianate style tower at the head of Main Street records the time. This station was designed by American-bred and trained architect Hugh Jones whose Montreal firm enjoyed a long association with the CPR. *(Bill Linley)*

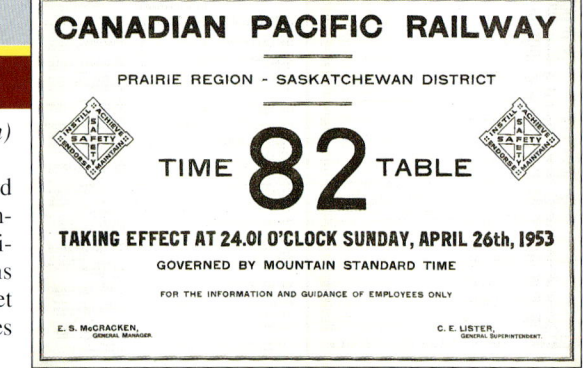

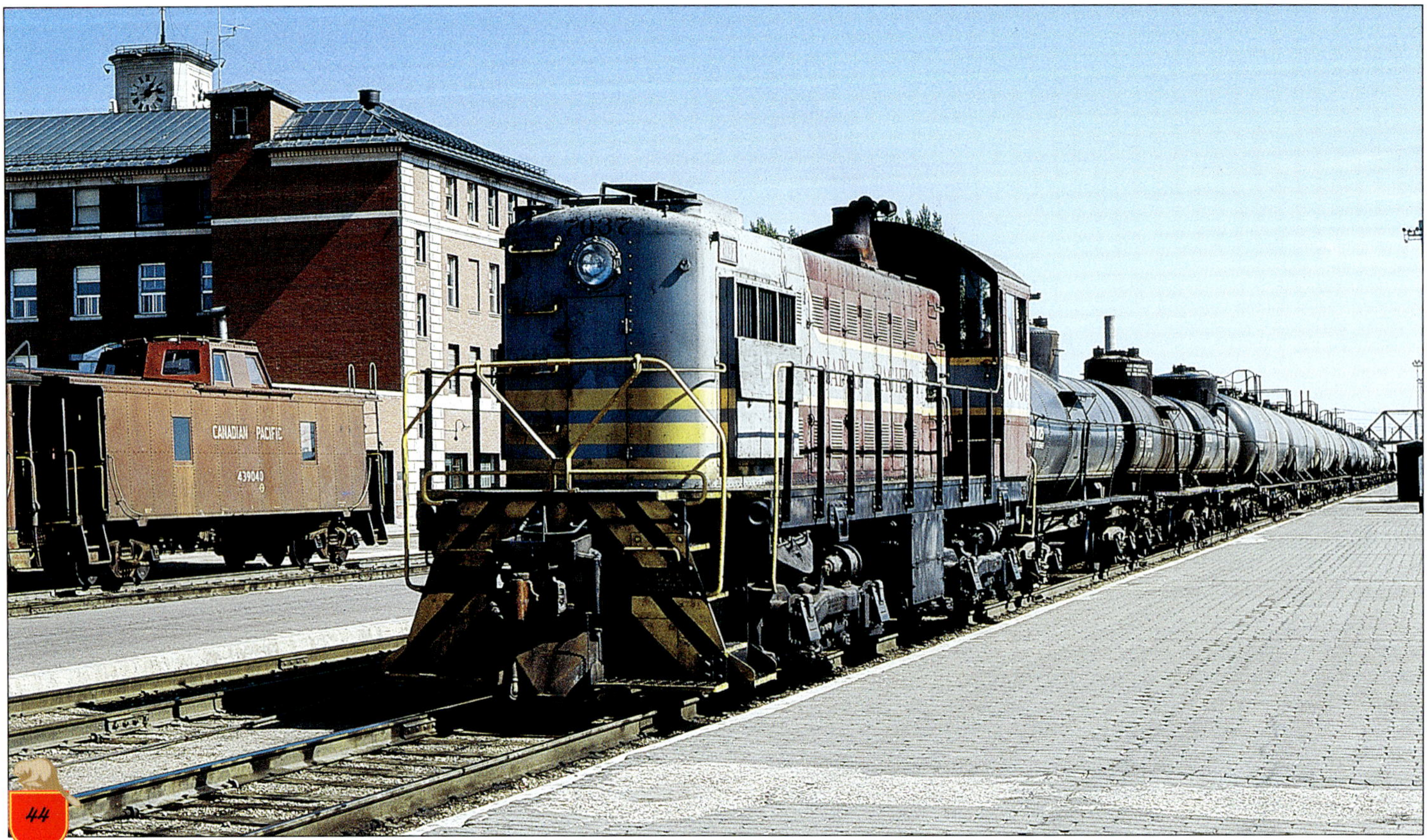

Above ⊕ Oil-burning class R3b Decapod 5762 was a January, 1918 product of the Angus Shops and is listed as an oil-burner throughout her long career. Assigned to Revelstoke in December 1952, with dieselization the engine has been transferred to switching duties at Moose Jaw where she is seen just east of the station on Tuesday morning, September 8, 1959. In 1952, Moose Jaw was home to 64 steamers, the third largest assignment of engines on the Western Lines. Two of CPR's 3 0-10-0's (Angus 10-1914) 6951 and 6952 were included. By May 1959, 48 steamers, 14 diesels and two RDC's were assigned. *(Robert Trennert)*

Above ⊕ G3f Pacific 2358 leads a westbound extra by the station tracks on Monday, August 31, 1959. This engine was assigned to 'AH', Alyth in Calgary, Alberta at the end of 1952. *(Keith Anderson)*

Right ⊕ G3g Pacific 2380 races east with a freight consist on a December, 1956 day en route to its assigned terminal in Moose Jaw. In April 1957 it would be assigned to Saskatoon for about a year of service on passenger runs to Regina.
(Robert Hale, Morning Sun Books Collection)

Above ◉ In the late summer of 1953, T1a class Selkirk 2-10-4 5906 (MLW 8-1929) powers an eastbound drag past the rural station at Ernfold, mileage 66.5 on the 110.4-mile Swift Current Sub in southern Saskatchewan. The Alyth-assigned Selkirk has only recently begun to run east of Calgary having been displaced from the mountainous Calgary – Revelstoke runs by the arrival of diesels in 1952. The 63" drivers, a 275-psi boiler and 25.5 x 32" cylinders combined to produce a tractive effort of 77,200 lbs on this oil-fired engine. A trailing-truck booster provided another 12,000 lbs of tractive effort at starting speeds. Although powerful, the small drivers of the Selkirks were ill suited to the high speeds of the Prairie mainlines and enjoyed only brief service lives North and East of Calgary. *(Ron Bearman)*

Above ◉ Brand new DFA-16e class FA-2 4087 blasts past Waldeck, mileage 99.3 on the last lap in to Swift Current in September 1953. Just 2.9 miles farther west, the junction at Baird accessed the 19.9 mile Stewart Valley Subdivision. The FA-2 emerged from MLW in Montreal on September 11 and this appears to be her maiden run to the west en route to assignment in Nelson, B.C. Rails on the Swift Current Sub were laid in 1882 as part of the original push to the Pacific Coast. *(Ron Bearman)*

Shaunavon Sub

Above ◉ In 1955, daily except Sunday Train 320 was scheduled to arrive at Assiniboia for a half hour stop at 1.55 p.m. having left Shaunavon at the west end of the 118.2 mile Shaunavon Sub at 9.45 a.m. Arrival in Moose Jaw was scheduled for 5.05 p.m. Wooden coach 335 was built just prior to World War I and seated 72 passengers. These coaches were used across the system in secondary service, notably in latter years for ski trains and picnic specials from terminals such as Winnipeg, Calgary and Lethbridge. In 1952 and again in October 1955, G2s Pacific's 2575 and 2533 were assigned to work Expanse Subdivision passenger trains from the Moose Jaw terminal of Train 320. This shot was taken between the summers of 1952 and 1955. *(Ron Bearman)*

Left and Below ◉ While serving as the CPR operator at Assiniboia, Ron Bearman also photographed D10k class Ten-wheeler 1078 (MLW 10-1912). Spotted in front of the station, the crew is enjoying lunch while in the accompanying view, a cut of cars is being moved through the yard. The cab curtains suggest a cold and windy day. Assiniboia was an important grain-collecting junction at the west (south) end of the 65.2-mile Expanse Sub that left the mainline at Curle, 2.3 miles west of Moose Jaw on the Swift Current Sub. To the east lay the Assiniboia Sub connection from Weyburn and to the south, the 79-mile Fife Lake Sub to Big Beaver that split off the Shaunavon Sub 1.9 miles west of Assiniboia at Ardwick. Sub-branches off the Fife Lake line included 24.6 miles of the Colony Sub from Rockglen mileage 36.3 to Killdeer and from Ogle, mileage 11.8, the Wood Mountain Sub 64.6 miles to Mankota. *(Two photos, Ron Bearman)*

SASKATOON DIVISION

Wynyard Sub

Above ⊕ At the eastern end of the 113.8-mile Wynyard Sub, at Bredenbury, Saskatchewan in June 1972, two sections of Edmonton – Winnipeg Train 976 change crews and prepare to depart for Minnedosa over the Bredenbury Sub. On the right, flying green, DRF-24b C-424 4219 (MLW 10-1965) will lead the first section. DRS-17b class GP9 8532 (GMDL 6-1955) leading leased Baltimore & Ohio F7's 4589 and 4487 waits on the left. Twenty-five units of the CPR's second order for GP9s, 8522 – 8546 were intended for Winnipeg – Saskatoon Trains 977 and 978 on this line as well as Winnipeg – Brandon – Calgary scheduled freights.
(Ken Goslett)

Left ⊕ D10g 922 (Angus 7-1911) switches van 436973 at Bredenbury on Thursday, June 11, 1959. Construction of the Winnipeg – Edmonton 'Prairie North Line' by CPR subsidiary Manitoba and Northwestern from Portage La Prairie began in the early 1880's. The line was completed to Minnedosa in 1884 and reached Bredenbury in the District of Assiniboia in 1889.
(R. S. Ritchie)

Left ⊕ HS-5b 12 (CLC 1-1958) was the switcher assigned to Yorkton, 26 miles west of Bredenbury on the 113.8-mile Wynyard Sub in August 1966. Manitoba and North Western's first train reached Yorkton from the east on January 9, 1891. A small city soon developed. In the background on Livingstone Street is the Balmoral Hotel, locally known as "The Bal," built in 1897 and once owned by Harry Bronfman of the Bronfman (Seagrams) dynasty. During prohibition in the 1920's, the hotel was associated with whiskey running and was rumoured to have tunnels linking it to the CPR freight shed for outward-bound shipments.
(John McIntosh, Bill Linley Collection)

Sutherland Sub

Above ⊕ The 'Prairie North Line' continued west for 113.5 miles from Wynyard to Saskatoon on the banks of the South Saskatchewan River. On Tuesday, August 3, 1965, Train 80 is at Lanigan, mileage 37.7 on its way to Wynyard, having completed its run from the yard at Sutherland, mileage 109.7, on the east side of the river at Saskatoon. DRS-17e class GP9 8805 was from the CPR's 1958 order for 23 units: 8801 - 8823; 8805 was delivered in January. *(John Rushton)*

Prince Albert Sub

Above ⊕ Saskatoon assigned D10g 908 (Angus 6-1911) arrives in Prince Albert with a northbound train from Lanigan on Thursday, September 3, 1959. The 908 was at Cranbrook, British Columbia in December 1952 and was displaced by dieselization. The 113.4-mile Prince Albert Sub from Lanigan was opened in 1930. Trackage rights were obtained on the CNR's Tisdale Sub for the final 19 route miles from Northway into Prince Albert. This CNR line from Prince Albert eastward to Hudson's Bay Junction had been opened by the Canadian Northern in 1905. *(Keith Anderson)*

Wilkie Sub

Top, Above and Below ⊕ Trains 975 and 976 between Winnipeg and Edmonton were scheduled to meet at Biggar, Saskatchewan, in September 1968. However, on Saturday the 28th, a late-running Train 975 caused the meet to be moved 32.6 miles east to a very rural, Urban, 27.6 miles west of Saskatoon. To make the meet, Train 976 powered by GP9's 8617, 8672, 8501, GP7 8419 and GP9 8490 has backed its train onto the beginning of the 43.8-mile Asquith Sub that continued to Baljennie. Fortunately, the subdivision's wayfreight, Trains 71 and 72 ran only on Wednesdays, so it was not on hand to complicate the movements. In time, Train 975 appears at track speed with 8483 leading three other GP9s, 8503, 8537, 8493 and RS-23, 8014. DRS-17a class 8483 is the CPR's first GP9, featuring the 567C engine producing 1750 horsepower and was outshopped on September 30, 1954. The through route via Macklin and Hardisty, Alberta opened in 1910. *(Three photos, Bill Linley)*

Canadian Pacific In Color

Cutknife Sub

Above ⊕ With 1000 horsepower RS-23 8014 (MLW 8-1959) leading, CP Train 93 arrives at CNR's North Battleford Station on the CNR's Blackfoot Subdivision around 5 p.m. on Tuesday September 16, 1969. Triweekly Trains 93 and 94 ran from Wilkie on the Winnipeg – Saskatoon – Wetaskawin line to North Battleford. The Lloydminster Sub through Cufknife – mileage 27.8 and reached in 1908 – opened for 104.3 miles from Wilkie to Lloydminster on the Alberta-Saskatchewan border in 1930. Train 93 was scheduled out of Wilkie at 15.00 for the hour long, 26.4- mile run to Cutoff on the Cutknife Sub. Three point five miles beyond Cutoff at Rosemound, joint track was used on CNR's Cut Knife Sub for 26.8 miles to Cut Knife Jct., then followed a 5.6 mile-long backup move on the CNR's Battleford Sub to Battleford Jct, and, finally, a further 6.1 miles eastward across the North Saskatchewan River on the CNR's Blackfoot Sub to North Battleford. Note the Watchman heater in front of 8014's cab that kept engine cooling water from freezing where heated engine houses were unavailable during weekend layovers. *(John Rushton)*

Meadow Lake Sub

Above ⊕ Mixed Train 656 is called for an 8.00 a.m. departure from Meadow Lake on Tuesday, February 23, 1971. On Tuesdays only, the train ran 55.1 miles east on the 93.4-mile Meadow Lake Sub to Panton were it joined the 36-mile Medstead Sub for Healy, 48.8 miles north of North Battleford. (The Medstead Sub opened in 1931.) At Healy, a joint track arrangement began with the CNR for the remaining miles into North Battleford. The CN routing was over the CNR's Robinhood Sub to Avery, from Avery to Prinham over the Hatherleigh Sub and finally from Prinham to North Battleford over the Turtleford Sub. The train would return the next day as Train 657. The leading RS-23's, 8018 and 8015, were part of MLW's 1959 6-unit answer to the need for lightweight units for branchlines such as these where the individual axle weight could not exceed 22.2 tons. Simplifications over the standard RS-23 to achieve the weight limits included the use of switcher-style 731-type traction motors, plain bearings and 750-gallon fuel tanks. *(Ken McCutcheon)*

Above ⊕ Train 656 is lifting pulpwood empties at Penn, mileage 41.1 of the Meadow Lake Sub at 10.40 a.m. on February 23, 1971. *(Ken McCutcheon)*

Above ⊕ Train 660 from Meadow Lake pauses for switching at Leoville, mileage 34.2 of the Meadow Lake line on Thursday, July 20, 1972. The portion east of Panton, mileage 38.3, received twice-weekly service directly to and from Prince Albert, eastbound on Thursday and Saturday and from westbound Trains 653 on Monday and Friday. Car 21301 was built at the Angus Shops in May 1914 as colonist car 2882, rebuilt as baggage-smoking combine 3313 in November 1956, and renumbered as a transfer caboose in July 1970. *(Doug Phillips)*

Above ⊕ Train 656 has reached the end of its 140-mile run from Meadow Lake at CNR's North Battleford Station on the afternoon of February 23, 1971. *(Ken McCutcheon)*

Pacific Region
Medicine Hat Division

Maple Creek Sub

Above ⊕ Vision Test Car 66 has recently arrived in Swift Current on Thursday, June 30, 1966 after a run over the 111.8 miles of the Empress Sub from Empress, Alberta. It is trailing the consist of the return run of daily except Sunday Swift Current – Leader – Burstall freight, Train 75, that also carried passengers. The car would have been switched from Empress – Leader – Fox Valley mixed Train 708 at Leader, Saskatchewan, 23.8 miles east of Empress. The Empress Sub was opened westwards from its junction at Java, mileage 5.6 of the Maple Creek Sub during the period 1911 through 1914. Vision test car 66 was built in August 1926 as the 10-compartment car Glen Finnian and converted to buffet sleeper Mattawa in August 1941 and to café sleeper Duncan (6 sections, 1 bedroom and 24 dining seats) in March 1952. With running mate, Dean, it served on overnight Calgary – Nelson Trains 541/67 and 68/542. From May 1960 it served as the vision test car on the Prairie and Pacific Regions. *(John MacIntosh, Bill Linley Collection)*

Right ⊕ Employee's Timetable. Note the effective time of 24.01, i.e. 12.01 a.m.
(Bill Linley Collection)

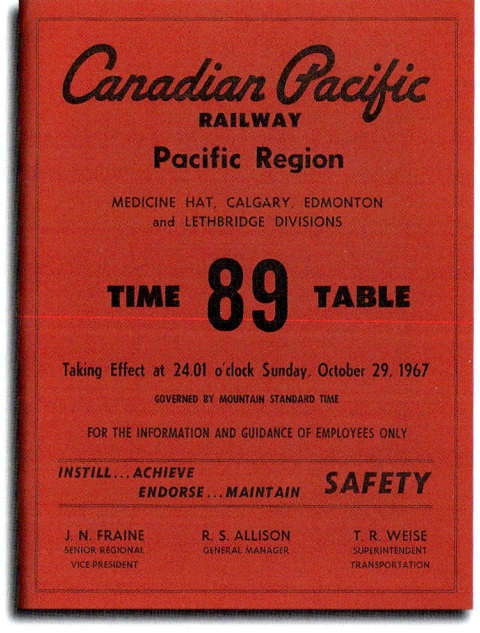

Below ⊕ Train 1, THE CANADIAN, passes Piapot, mileage 67.1 on the 147.4-mile Maple Creek Sub through the drylands of southwestern Saskatchewan on Saturday, May 21, 1966. FP9 1407 left Swift Current at 8.00 a.m. having made the change from Central to Mountain Standard Time. (As of the fall change of time on October 29, 1961, the Railway moved the locale for its change of Central to Mountain time from Broadview two divisions west to Swift Current.) The next stop is a flag stop at Maple Creek, Saskatchewan for revenue passengers at 9.29 a.m. with a projected 10.36 a.m. arrival in Medicine Hat, Alberta at the west end of the subdivision. The Maple Creek Sub opened in 1883 as part of the original mainline to the Pacific. *(Keith Anderson)*

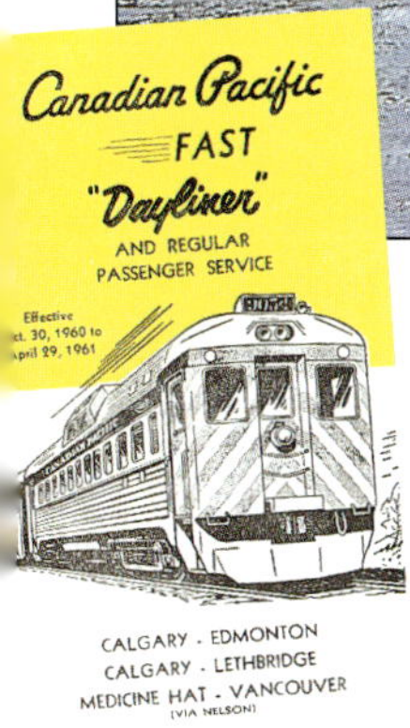

Brooks Subdivision

Above ⊕ On arrival in Medicine Hat, Alberta, in December 1961, THE CANADIAN met a connecting, daily *Dayliner* service for Nelson, British Columbia and beyond to Vancouver. Seventy-seat RDC-2 9100, CPR's initial RDC-2 (Budd 3-1955), sits in the "Crow-Main" pocket track to the east of the station awaiting its departure at 9.55 a.m. (Behind it sits the superintendent's business car number 16 (Barney & Smith 1890) which is now on display as the *British Columbia* at the West Coast Railway Heritage Park in Squamish, B.C.) Arrival in Nelson is scheduled for 9.45 p.m. On the following Monday and Thursday mornings, at 9.00 a.m., Train 45 would continue on to Spences Bridge to connect with Train 7, THE DOMINION, at 12.30 a.m. for a second morning arrival in Vancouver. The CPR introduced Budd's versatile self-propelled car to Canada in 1953 and acquired North America's second largest fleet that it used from Nova Scotia to Vancouver Island. *(Keith Anderson)*

Left ⊕ "*Dayliner*" schedule for Alberta services as well as the service through Nelson to Vancouver. *(Gerry Gaugl Collection)*

Left ⊕ Just after the departure of Train 307, Keith Anderson found DS-9a class 900-horsepower, SW900 6720 idling at the Medicine Hat enginehouse. 900-horsepower 6720 was CPR's last GMDL switcher (4-1955) and was ordered in 1954 along with ten others to complement the earlier SW8's and SW9's already in service in the Pacific Region. The eleven units were distributed to Edmonton, Alyth and Kamloops with 6713 going to Medicine Hat. Note the classification lights on the engine, as the unit and sister 6719 would be used from time to time as pushers east to Dunmore and west to Redcliff or Bowell. *(Keith Anderson)*

Above ⊕ Over a decade later on Friday, March 26, 1971, THE CANADIAN has departed at 11.15 a.m. and RDC-2 9195 (Canadian Car & Foundry 9-1957) has backed into the station ready to depart at 11.40 a.m. as Train 307. By this time, service through Southern British Columbia had ended and Train 307 would terminate at Lethbridge at 1.40 p.m. after traveling almost all of the 107.7 miles of the Taber Sub. The initial portion of the trip would be eastbound on the Maple Creek Sub to Macson, five miles southeast of Medicine Hat and the wye connection to Roytal, 2.1 miles west of Dunmore where the Taber Sub joined the Maple Creek Sub. The portion of the Maple Creek Sub between Medicine Hat and Macson saw CPR's first installation of CTC signaling. The system was installed in 1928 and featured General Railway Signal semaphore signals and a power switch to enter the main track from the east end of Medicine Hat yard and another power switch at the west end of Dunmore. Medicine Hat to Lethbridge passenger trains were still required to use a hand-thrown turnout in order to utilize the wye connection between Macson and Roytal in the initial arrangement of this early CTC system.

(Ken McCutcheon)

Left ⊕ With malfunctioning injectors on GP9 8513, a smoky eastbound 'fertilizer turn' to the Western Co-operative Fertilizer plant west of Shepard surmounts the Ogden Escarpment, a few miles east of Calgary on Labor Day, September 1, 1969. In June 1965, GP9's 8661-8671, 8675-8679 and 8681-8685 were involved in ongoing tests using a very light Lloydminster crude oil that was simply filtered and de-watered. These Geeps did not smoke as heavily as the 8513 in this view. Similarly, a six-month test was conducted on C-424's 4247 – 4250 in 1971 using "synthetic" crude from the Athabaska Tar Sands. The low viscosity of the crude allowed the same fuel to be used throughout the year.

(Doug Phillips)

Left ⊕ Near the west end of the Brooks Sub, at mileage 168.6, Train 1st 944 is on its way from Vancouver to North Portal Saskatchewan and the Soo Line connection with FP7 4034 leading GP9s 8494, 8616 and 8517 at 9.04 a.m. Sunday, March 5, 1972. *(Bob Loat)*

Langdon Sub

Above ⊕ GP9 8663 leads northbound Train 67 at Keoma, mileage 18.5 on Monday, August 5, 1968. The train is headed for Wimborne on the 27.3-mile Acme Sub that opened in 1930 and branched off the Langdon Sub at Cosway, mileage 41.7. The 94.3-mile Langdon Sub branched off the Strathmore Sub – the original mainline of 1883 – at mileage 33.7, 1.1 miles east of Langdon. The train originated at Alyth Yard in Calgary, mileage 173.3 of the Brooks Sub and had traveled east to Shepard, mileage 165.6.

At Shepard, the 45.1-mile old mainline looped north through Langdon and Strathmore to rejoin the Brooks Sub at Gleichen, mileage 124.8. Between Shepard and Gleichen, a 39.8-mile cutoff opened as part of the Brooks Sub in 1914. The Langdon Sub reached Acme, mileage 39.8, by 1910 and was extended in 1921 and 1923 to Kneehill, mileage 78.7 and East Coulee in 1928. By 1930, the line had been extended a further 53.6 miles as the Rosemary Sub to Rosemary, 17.3 miles east of Bassano, mileage 97.6 of the Brooks Sub. *(Bob Loat)*

Empress Sub

Above ⊕ Mileage 107, five miles east of Empress marks the crossing of the South Saskatchewan River as its tributary, the Red Deer River, joins just to the right of the frame. Conductor Charlie Monk is in charge on Monday, September 24, 1974 as an eastbound empty pipe train powered by GP9 8536 is headed from Empress, Alberta to Swift Current and is approaching Estuary, Saskatchewan. *(Doug Phillips)*

Bassano Sub

Above ⊕ GP9 8837 stands at Empress with an eastbound train on Monday, June 16, 1969. Train orders were often issued at this time of year to trains to "watch out for rattlesnakes around switchstands Empress yard." The Bassano Sub opened over the 118.4 miles from Empress to Bassano in 1914 effectively extending the Empress Sub to form a loop to the north of the original main line. This effort by CPR President Lord Shaughnessy was part of a double tracking program in the west and was specifically intended to bypass the steep grades in and out of Medicine Hat. *(Doug Phillips)*

Irricana Sub

Above ⊕ Due to a washout between Tudor and Irricana, Work Extra 8691 has turned on the wye at Standard, mileage 35.8 of the Irricana Sub on Friday, November 24, 1974 and will gather further grain boxes on its return trip to Bassano. This 72.2-mile line reached Standard from Irricana, mileage 26.2 of the Langdon Sub, in 1911 and continued to Bassano on the Brooks Sub in 1912. *(Doug Phillips)*

EDMONTON DIVISION

Above ◉ Train 302 pauses for the three-minute stop at the division point of Red Deer in September 1967. The station opened in 1910. The Alpha Dairy of the Central Alberta Dairy Pool is in the background. *(Richard Yaremko)*

Leduc Sub

Above ◉ M4a Consolidation 3409 takes a brief break from switching duties at Strathcona on the South Side of the North Saskatchewan River on Saturday, July 27, 1957. CPR's main Edmonton freight yard was located in South Edmonton, mileage 96.9 of the Leduc Sub and 2.2 miles south of the Edmonton station. The 2-8-0 (MLW 11-1904) was equipped with 21x28" cylinders, 58" drivers and a 200 psi boiler giving a tractive effort of 36,200 pounds. This engine was a member of the first class built new as superheated locomotives and was originally equipped with Stephenson (slide-valve) gear which was subsequently converted to Walschaerts, the CPR's standard. It was scrapped in December 1957. *(John Mills)*

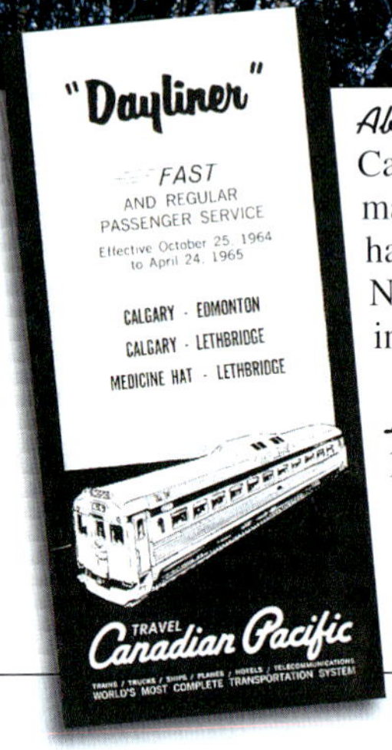

Above ⊕ The High Level Bridge over the North Saskatchewan River opened in 1913 and replaced trackage rights over the Canadian Northern's (CNR) low-level bridge. Southbound Train 302, THE STAMPEDER, due to depart at 1.30 p.m. is normally assigned *Dayliners,* however, holiday traffic has dictated a conventional train and a pair of boiler-equipped GP9s has drawn the assignment on Saturday, January 2, 1965. The provincial legislature may be seen to the right of 8512. Note the rails still in place for streetcars that kept to the left across the bridge so that passengers could safely disembark in the event of an emergency prior to the abandonment of the system in September 1951. *(Peter Cox)*

Left ⊕ The somber colors of this schedule for Alberta *Dayliners* matched those of the system timetable in the fall of 1964. *(Gerry Gaugl Collection)*

Below ⊕ A family enjoys 'watch the birdie' on Sunday afternoon, September 8, 1963 at the Edmonton Station as RDC-2 9198 and RDC-1 9055 form the background. Train 302, THE STAMPEDER, will depart at 1.30 p.m. The station at 109th Street and Athabaska Avenue immediately west of downtown opened in 1913. *(Peter Cox)*

CALGARY DIVISION

Left ⊕ At Bengal, Train 302 has just entered the two-track segment south of the Bow River that continues for 1.2 miles to the junction at 12th Street East with the Calgary Terminals Sub. In a further 1.3 miles, at 12.10 p.m., on Sunday, November 27, 1970, dual-service GP9 8512 will come to a stop at the Calgary station to connect with THE CANADIAN's. Uniquely for CPR GP9s, 8511 and 8512 had been equipped with 89 mph gearing from 1960 through 1965 for the occasional operation of conventional trains on the Edmonton – Calgary route when fish traffic was offered. They were kept in this area and also operated on THE DOMINION to Winnipeg and as third units on THE CANADIAN from Calgary to Revelstoke. *(Doug Phillips)*

Red Deer Sub

Left ⊕ Calgary – Edmonton Train 987 crosses Nose Creek just north of Calgary around 1.00 p.m. on Saturday, April 19, 1969 behind C-424 4210, F7B 4424 and FP7 4036. The Calgary and Edmonton Railway, which the CPR leased in 1905, completed the 93.5 miles of the CPR's Red Deer Sub from Calgary to Red Deer in 1891. *(Doug Phillips)*

Below ⊕ Train Masters 8917 and 8909 head a northbound Crossfield Turn (mileage 28.9) pulling by the 110-car siding at Beddington, mileage 8.8. Stan Smaill caught the scene in September 1969. The empties would carry sulphur on their return from the gas plants near Crossfield. *(Stan Smaill)*

Above ⊕ At Carstairs, Train 304 is en route from Edmonton to Calgary at 11.33 a.m. on Monday, September 23, 1968. RDC-2 9195 (Budd / CC&F 5-1958) is equipped with bars on the front windows to ward off the effects of too many meets with errant prairie fowl. The six RDC-2's in the 9194 – 9199 series were separated from the 17 cars beginning at 9100 due to the three-seat reduction to 68 seats associated with the installation of a second washroom in late model RDC-2s. All CPR RDC-2's had a 17' baggage compartment. In the background, the elevator touting the Alberta Pacific Grain Company, together with those of the Seale Grain Company had passed into the hands of Federal Grain Limited in 1967. *(Bill Linley)*

Above ⊕ GP9 8632 and H16-44 8714 motor north with Calgary – Edmonton Train 987 at Carstairs in August 1969, just south of the station at mileage 40.7. *(Stan Smaill)*

Above ⊕ The Red Deer Sub wayfreight has just passed the 1902-era mansard-roofed Didsbury station as designed by company architect R.B. Pratt. GP9 8838 is about to exit the passing track seven miles north of Carstairs and continue south in July 1970. *(Richard Yaremko)*

Above ⊕ Northbound Train 301 with two coaches and a baggage car serving as a buffer car occupies the siding at Innisfail as the employee timetable indicates that it is operating in the inferior direction. To minimize train delays, Train 301 will back out of the siding and resume its trip once Train 302 with RDC-2's 9113 and 9105 has passed on its way to Calgary on Saturday, December 29, 1973. Running 30 minutes late at 10.24 a.m., northbound Train 302 with two coaches and a baggage car serving as a buffer car occupies the siding at Innisfail, mileage 75.2, as the employee timetable indicates that it is operating in the inferior direction. The dispatcher has changed the meet from Tuttle, mileage 89.1, and to minimize train delays Train 301 will back out of the siding and resume its trip once Train 302 with RDC-2s 9113 and 9105 has passed on its way to Calgary on Saturday, December 29, 1973. The temperature was –25 degrees Fahrenheit. *(Doug Phillips)*

Right ◉ On Saturday, March 14, 1970, GP9 8677 is on the last lap into Calgary with the Acme-Langdon Sub wayfreight, including a sulphur tank from the Wimborne spur as it passes the Ogden Shops. The shops opened in 1913 for car and locomotive repairs on the Pacific Region.
(*Doug Phillips*)

Calgary Terminals

Right ◉ FA-2 4087 and an FB-1 lift eastbound Train 96, a Medicine Hat bound advance section of Calgary – Montreal – Saint John Train 952, 'The Seaboard' at the 50th Avenue crossing just east of Alyth Yard shortly after 4.00 p.m. on Tuesday, March 23, 1965. To make better time in the fall stock rush, traffic would sometimes run to Swift Current via the Bassano and Empress subs instead of following the mainline Brooks and Maple Creek subs. (*Peter Cox*)

Below ◉ Looking east from the Alyth Yard overbridge on Tuesday, July 23, 1957, N2a Consolidation 3650 is pulling a cut of cars toward the connection with the Red Deer Sub at the west end of Alyth Yard. The 2-8-0 was built at Angus in April 1909 with 23x32" cylinders, 63" drivers a 190 psi boiler yielding 43,400 lbs of tractive effort and was based in Revelstoke in 1952. Many N2a's became P1n Mikados in the late 1940's. The 36-stall Alyth Roundhouse appears behind the engine. A new diesel shop at Alyth opened in 1951 coincident with the beginnings of dieselization on the Calgary to Revelstoke main line. (*John Mills*)

Above ⊕ Looking west from the bridge, CP V5a class 0-8-0 6965 pulls back with a pair of vans on the same July day. Normally assigned to work the Alyth Hump, the switcher had been renumbered from the 6606 in January 1957 to make way for additional MLW switchers and would remain on the roster until scrapped in September 1965. Note 2-8-0 3650 in the upper right of the photo. The double track completed on the left in 1914 ran from Ogden on the Brooks Sub to Sunalta on the Laggan Sub west of Calgary. *(John Mills)*

Left ⊕ Edmonton – Calgary Train 988 was scheduled to arrive at Alyth Yard at 2.00 p.m. on Tuesday, September 24, 1968, after its 9.5 hour run. The lead unit is MLW C-424 4221 trailed by GMDL GP35 5003 and F7B 4462. MLW FA-2 4044 was traded-in on the C-424 that was delivered in October 1965 while the GP35 was built in May 1964 as the 8203. *(Bob Loat)*

Above ⊕ C-630M 4503, class DRF-30c, leads a trio of SD40's at 12th Street Tower and is about to depart for a run over the Laggan Sub to Field, British Columbia. The 3000 hp unit was delivered in August 1968 as one of eight built by MLW to Alco designs in Montreal. They were the last units delivered in the tuscan and grey scheme and were purchased with Canadian designed hi-adhesion trucks as an antidote to the wheel-slip control and adhesion problems of the 65 SD40s. These MLW units re-used the GE-752 traction motors from retired Train Masters. *(Clayton Jones)*

Above ⊕ Near the 12th Street East interlocking tower at 10.45 a.m. on Sunday, December 19, 1971, GP9 8635 displays the first low nose conversion crafted at Ogden Shops a year earlier in anticipation of its use on the hump at Alyth Yard. The improved visibility would eliminate the need for a yardman in the cab. *(Bob Loat)*

Right ⊕ The corporate beaver was featured in a dining car menu for young travelers in the 1950's. *(Gerry Gaugl Collection)*

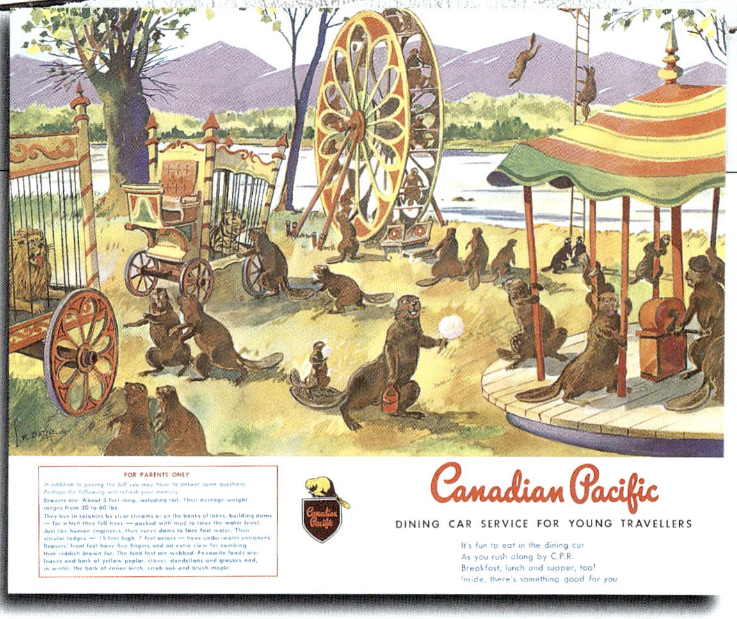

Right ⊕ On an afternoon in April, 1969, the westbound CANADIAN has just passed 12th Street East tower at the west end of Alyth Yard and in a few minutes will arrive at the Calgary Station. The interlocking tower was the junction with the MacLeod Sub to the south and the Red Deer Sub to the north. *(John Riddell)*

Right Center ⊕ Saturday-only Train 718, the *'Wimborne Mixed,'* dubbed the *'Acme Mixed'* by train crews, nears the Calgary station minutes before the scheduled arrival time of 2.20 p.m. on October 22, 1960. GP9 8539 will have completed the 89.6-mile trip in the scheduled seven hours and twenty minutes. The first 27.3 miles traveled were over the Acme Sub from Wimborne to Cosway that opened in 1930. At Cosway, Train 718 entered the Langdon Sub at mileage 41.7 and continued on to Calgary over the Strathmore and Brooks Subdivisions. *(Bob Sandusky)*

Below ⊕ The photographer's son, three year old Trevor, keeps his eyes on the power as THE CANADIAN awaits its 3.05 p.m. departure from the Calgary Station on Saturday, June 1, 1968. A 1937-vintage baggage-express boxcar in the 4900 – 4910 series is painted to match THE CANADIAN's consist and usually ran from Calgary to Vancouver carrying bulk Royal Mail such as magazines. In the background stands the company's Palliser Hotel, opened in 1914 with 350 rooms as designed in the Edwardian Commercial Style with a Chicago look by architect Lawrence Gotch. *(Bob Loat)*

Left ⊕ Winter Timetable 1967 *(Bill Linley Collection)*

Below ⊕ GP9s 8681 and 8650 are spliced by F7B's 4439 and 4448 at 3rd Street West as an Extra East passes the site of the recently removed coach yard as it approaches the west end of the station on Sunday morning, October 22, 1967. Robin Hood Flour Mills Ltd's. elevator in the background remained active until 1969 as a highly visible sign that *Robin Hood* was Canada's leading consumer brand of flour. Its removal allowed the construction of Gulf Canada Square that would become the headquarters for the Canadian Pacific Railway in 1996. *(Bob Loat)*

Above ⊕ At 9.00 a.m. on Saturday, September 23, 1967, the Expo Limited has entered the fall of its brief reincarnation of The Dominion as the CPR's secondary transcontinental passenger run. The last run will occur with the change back to Standard Time on October 28. National Steel Car/Angus built (5-1950) 10-5 sleeper *Poplar Grove* is deadheading on Train 5. On this cloudless day, the car washer, installed in 1955 with the debut of The Canadian, is running and the train is sparkling as it departs for the vistas of the Canadian Rockies. In the background, the 626-foot Husky (Oil) Tower beside the Palliser Hotel will be completed by June 30, 1968. *(Bob Loat)*

Laggan Sub

Left ⊕ A '*Keith Turn*' heads west at mileage 3.5 of the Laggan Sub along the Bow River on the western outskirts of Calgary on Sunday, January 25, 1970. Train Masters 8909, 8917 and 8903, of the seven remaining at the time, provide the power on this train of grain loads which will be dropped at mileage 9.6, Keith, an assembly yard for filling out drag freights destined for the West Coast. *(Bob Loat)*

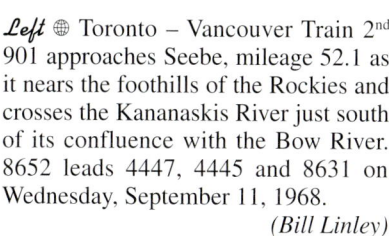

Left ⊕ Toronto – Vancouver Train 2nd 901 approaches Seebe, mileage 52.1 as it nears the foothills of the Rockies and crosses the Kananaskis River just south of its confluence with the Bow River. 8652 leads 4447, 4445 and 8631 on Wednesday, September 11, 1968.

(Bill Linley)

Below ⊕ GP9 8667 leads a quartet of Geeps on 1st 950 from Vancouver to Calgary at The Gap, just west of Exshaw on Sunday, October 29, 1967. Lougheed Mountain at 10,154 feet dominates the scene. A track relocation here yielded a soft granite rock that was used to ballast Alyth Yard two miles east of the station in Calgary. *(Bob Loat)*

Left ● SW9 class DS-12a 7404 (GMDL 3-1953) hurries away from the Mountain Observation Car on the tail end of Train 13, THE MOUNTAINEER from St. Paul via Portal and Moose Jaw on a July day in 1953. As headlights were not required for daytime running at this time, the illumination on GP7 8411 suggests that Train 2, the all-stops transcontinental local, is falling behind its scheduled 10.10 departure from the Banff station. The six SW9's were the CPR's only 1200-horsepower GM switchers and shortly after delivery were exchanged for MLW S-4's 7109-7114 for the Kootenay and Kettle Valley lines and were assigned to Field, Revelstoke and work trains including snowplows upon the dieselization of the Laggan and Mountain Subs. *(Dr. H.R. Blackburn, Morning Sun Books Collection)*

Above ● Train 7, THE DOMINION, pauses at Banff at 11.35 a.m. on Monday, September 17, 1951. THE DOMINION's Toronto section, Train 3 had departed at 11.20 a.m. and Train 13, THE MOUNTAINEER, at 10.35. Many passengers were handled at Banff in the heart of the Canadian Rockies and site of such world-famous attractions as Banff National Park and the CPR's Banff Springs Hotel. T1b class Selkirk 5926 was built at MLW in November, 1938 with 63" drivers, 25x32" cylinders and a 285 psi boiler yielding 76,900 pounds of tractive effort excluding a further 12,500 pounds from a trailing-truck booster. *(R. S. Ritchie)*

Right ● The cover of the 1953 edition of the 28-page guide to the mainline through the Rockies emphasized the new diesel power on the Calgary – Revelstoke run. In May 1952, a special train was run from Montreal to Field and return to gather still and movie images in the newly dieselized territory. Company photographer Nicholas Morant lensed two-month-old FP7 4062 with F7B 4446 at Massive near mileage 93 along the banks of the Bow River. 4062 would become 1420 in January 1955 in preparation for the inauguration of THE CANADIAN. *(Bill Linley Collection)*

Above ⊕ The eastbound CANADIAN swoops around Morant's Curve, mileage 113 of the Laggan Sub about 2.20 p.m. on Saturday, March 28, 1964. Photographer Peter Cox was part of a group of West Coast Railway Association members that had traveled to Golden aboard THE DOMINION and transferred to a chartered Brewster Lines MCI Courier 85 to motorcade their DOMINION, THE CANADIAN and other trains en route to Banff on the Easter Holiday weekend. Morant's Curve along the Bow River was made famous by CPR staff-photographer Nicholas Morant (1910-1999) who featured the sweeping S-curve in many of his images. Fairview Mountain (9, 011 feet) is above the lead FP7, the 4040 that lacks the icicle breakers common to the normally assigned 1400 series passenger-service FP's. *(Peter Cox)*

Above ⊕ Snowplow 401036 was built in 1952 and is seen at the East Switch at Lake Louise on Sunday, December 20, 1970 leading an eastbound Plow Extra powered by GP9 8654. *(Bob Loat)*

Above ⊕ A 1958 equipment brochure for THE CANADIAN also featured Morant's Curve. *(Gerry Gaugl Collection)*

Above ● "Life beyond death" applies to the EXPO LIMITED in this view at 12.08 p.m. on Sunday, October 29, 1967 as the train did not appear in Employee Timetable #89 taking effect at 24.01 (12.01 a.m.) that morning. Operating as a Passenger Extra West through to Vancouver, the train would be followed at Lake Louise by another two through trains from Montreal before the final curtain would close on the CPR's secondary transcontinental passenger service. Bumpers on the two 'garden tracks' formerly used for storing sleeping cars in the summer season protect the station. The log-station built in 1910 was one of a handful on the system and was well suited to its location in Banff National Park near the Railway's Chateau Lake Louise resort hotel. *(Bob Loat)*

Above ● Train 69 passes the station gardens at Lake Louise, mileage 116.6 on Saturday, August 2, 1969. SD40's 5558, 5529 and 5538 are in charge of this evening westbound run. The twenty miles beyond to Field on the other side of the Continental Divide opened in 1884 as the CPR pushed towards the Pacific Coast. Just ahead lays five miles of 1% grades to Stephen. The maximum encountered would be 2.2%. Lake Louise was renamed from Laggan in 1910 in honor of Princess Louise Caroline Alberta the fourth daughter of Queen Victoria. In 1905 the new province of Alberta was also named for Princess Louise. *(Doug Phillips)*

Left ● The EXPO LIMITED passes the East Switch at Stephen behind boiler-equipped GP9's 8514 and 8512 on Sunday afternoon, September 22, 1967. Just ahead at the British Columbia border was Divide, where a cairn marked the summit of the Rockies at 5,326 feet, the highest point on the CPR mainline. *(Bill Linley Collection)*

Above ⊕ A westbound freight runs beside Sink Lake, British Columbia, in the Kicking Horse Pass, behind DFA-16b class CPA16-4 4057 and a pair of CLC B-units in November 1952. 4057 was the last of six ordered as A-B sets from the Canadian Locomotive Company in 1951 for the dieselization of the Calgary to Revelstoke mainline. With the arrival of additional FP7's in 1952, 4057 and its Fairbanks-Morse designed 1600 hp mates were re-assigned from Alyth to Nelson for use in the Kootenay-Kettle Valley dieselization. The steam generator was removed in March 1963. *(Nicholas Morant, Omer Lavallee Collection)*

Right ⊕ On the final ascent to the Continental Divide, Train 902 runs out of the sag known as the 'Hector Dip' along Blue Creek just east of the former siding at Hector, mileage 125, with a quartet of SD40's 5511-5556-5544-5564 on Saturday, August 2, 1969. The third unit has an experimental CNR-style snow-shield above the air-intakes. Daily Vancouver – Toronto Train 902 had left Coquitlam at 8.45 p.m. on Friday, departed Field at 5.45 p.m. and was due in Toronto at 9.15 a.m. Tuesday. The 86.5 hour schedule made 902 the CPR's hottest transcontinental freight.

(Doug Phillips)

Above ⊕ Train 965 (Toronto – Vancouver) with a trio of Train Masters led by the 8916 meets Extra East 8907 at Hector on the south side of Wapta Lake, British Columbia. This view on Sunday, September 2, 1962 is from the shoulder of the Trans-Canada Highway, just east of the site of the CPR's Wapta Lake Lodge. To the south of the right-of-way is Narao Peak, 9,758 feet. Narao is a Stoney Indian word for "hit in the stomach," likely referring to surveyor James Hector being kicked by a horse in 1858 while traveling down the Kicking Horse River that empties Wapta Lake to the west. *(Peter Cox)*

Above ⊕ DRF-30b SD40 5541 leads DRF-30c C-630M 4500 at the site of the west switch at Hector on the 14.5-mile descent down the 2.2% grade of Field Hill from Stephen to Field. The date is Wednesday, June 24, 1970; 10,125-foot Mount Richardson dominates the left background. *(Clayton Jones)*

Above ⊕ Second 901 exits the Upper Spiral Tunnel in Cathedral Mountain while descending Field Hill at the west mileboard for Partridge on Wednesday, September 11, 1968. Partridge, mileage 127.8 is at the east portal of the Upper Spiral Tunnel. Just ahead the train will pass Yoho, formerly an 86-car intermediate siding between the two spiral tunnels. The floodplain of the Kicking Horse River, the Trans-Canada Highway and the CPR mainline at Cathedral may be seen far below. *(Bill Linley)*

Right ⊕ THE CANADIAN, Train 2, passes the East Switch at Yoho on Sunday, September 24, 1967, powered by 1418, 1903 and 1403. The icicle breakers and oscillating, roof-mounted Mars light that announced the nighttime approach of THE CANADIAN are clearly visible. In the background is Mount Ogden (8,842 feet) through which passes the 2,910 foot Lower Spiral Tunnel in three-quarters of a circle. *(Bob Loat)*

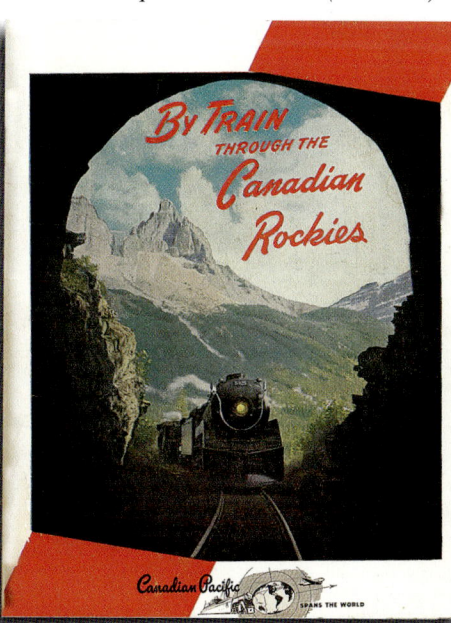

Left, Below ⊕ This twenty-four-page guide from the 1940's highlighted the westward trip from Morley, Alberta to Kamloops, B.C. and featured Selkirk 5925 about to enter the upper portal of the Lower Spiral Tunnel. Cathedral Crags at 10,081 feet towers high above the westbound train.
(Gerry Gaugl Collection)

Above ⊕ In May 1966 GP9 8806 leads an eastbound quartet of Geeps and a long string of boxcars still exiting the upper portal of the Lower Spiral Tunnel as it nears Yoho, mileage 129.8.

The Spiral Tunnels were opened on September 1, 1909 to replace the 4.4% grade of 1884 that dropped from Hector, B.C. to Field.

(Ray Matthews)

Above ⊕ This is the classic view of the Spiral Tunnels as seen from the look-off on the Trans-Canada Highway. On Saturday, August 5, 1967 Train 2 THE CANADIAN crosses the Kicking Horse River on its ascent to the Upper Spiral Tunnel where it will follow another three-quarter-circle cut through Cathedral Mountain.

The press for the 48 available seats in the two Budd domes would have been considerable as CPR's 36-car fleet of such cars precluded the use of multiple domes for almost all of its ownership of the train.

(Clayton Jones)

Above ⊕ Another A-B-A set leads Train 1 through the 'Nose Tunnel' and a snowshed along the side of Cathedral Mountain on the final descent to Field. FP7 1421 leads the way on Sunday, May 19, 1963. *(Peter Cox)*

Above ⊕ S2a Santa Fe 5811 pilots the Selkirk road engine on Train 8, the Montreal section of THE DOMINION just east of Field at 3.35 p.m. on Monday, September 17, 1951. The 2-10-2 was built by the Angus Shops in May 1920 with 58" drivers, 26.5x32" cylinders and a 200 psi boiler yielding a tractive effort of 65,900 pounds. *(R. S. Ritchie)*

Above ⊕ *Eastbound through the Canadian Rockies* was offered for sale at thirty-five cents. It was published by the CPR's News Department in 1947 and provided a detailed description of the line between Vancouver and Calgary.
(Gerry Gaugl Collection)

LETHBRIDGE DIVISION

Above ⊕ Train 14, the MOUNTAINEER, is scheduled to leave Field at 1.50 p.m. on a July day in 1952 and is approaching the East Switch behind class T1b-class Selkirk 5926. Coupled ahead is an A-A set of FP7s including 4032 newly returned from GMDL where a steam generator had been added in anticipation of its role in helper service. *(William McChesney, Morning Sun Books Collection)*

Taber Sub

Above ⊕ Trailing sugar beet loads, DRS-17c class GP9 8624 passes the east switch at Tempest, mileage 94.1 of the Taber Sub on the way to Alberta's only sugar beet refinery at Taber, mileage 76.5. It's 1.05 p.m. on Saturday, October 2, 1971. The Rogers Sugar Ltd. plant opened in 1950 and subsequently replaced earlier facilities at Picture Butte and Raymond. Beets grew successfully on the irrigated, semi-arid lands in the surrounding area as a result of the activities of the St. Maries Irrigation District and the Lethbridge Northern Irrigation District built by the Alberta Railway and Irrigation Company prior to the CPR take over in 1912. The North Western Coal and Navigation Co. opened the Dunmore – Lethbridge line in 1885 to supply Lethbridge coal to the CPR. The CPR leased the line in 1893, converted it to standard gauge and purchased it 1897.
(Bob Loat)

Crowsnest Sub

Right ⊕ Angus Shops turned out U3d class 0-6-0 6245 in June 1912 with 52" drivers, 18 x 26" cylinders, a 200-psi boiler and 27,500 pounds of tractive effort. On Monday, June 15, 1953, the switcher handles a van in front of the icehouse just west of the station in Lethbridge.

Below ⊕ On the same day in Lethbridge, Medicine Hat-assigned Mikado 5141 departs eastbound for its home terminal. P1e 2-8-2 (MLW 8 -1913) had 63" drivers, 23 x 32" cylinders, a 190-psi boiler and a tractive effort of 43,400 pounds. *(Two photos, R. S. Ritchie)*

Above ⊕ THE VULCAN, Train 311, had departed Lethbridge for Calgary at 9.00 a.m. on Sunday, January 22, 1961. Its 126.5-mile, two hour and forty minute trip would be via Coalhurst, mileage 6.4 of the Crowsnest Sub and then the Aldersyde Sub connecting to the MacLeod Sub at Aldersyde. The RDC-2 is crossing the 12,600-ton, 5,329-foot long High Level trestle some 314 feet above the Oldman River on the western edge of Lethbridge. The longest railway bridge in Canada opened on October 23, 1909 with the construction of a new line between Lethbridge and Fort MacLeod replacing the original alignment opened in 1898 as part of the Company's new line to Crowsnest on the British Columbia border.
(Bob Sandusky)

Left ⊕ Train 979 heads west into a frigid prairie sunset west of Fort MacLeod on Sunday, January 26, 1975. Traffic was lifted at Coalhurst from Train 992 from Calgary. At Cranbrook, traffic would be sorted for Kingsgate and Tadanac. *(Doug Phillips)*

Below ⊕ DRS-18b class RS-18 8781 (MLW 5-1958) leads Train 70 through the reverse curves east of Pincher, mileage 61.1, of the Crowsnest Sub on Wednesday, May 1, 1974. The newly developed RS-18 equipped with the new 1800 hp, Alco 251B V-12 debuted on the CPR in 1957 with an order for twenty units. The first ten, 8729 – 8738 were initially assigned to Chapleau for operation on fast freights on the Prairie Region from Fort William to Winnipeg. An additional 52 units were purchased in 1958 to complete the dieselization of through freights in the Eastern Region.
(Andrew Sutherland, Bruce Chapman Collection)

Above ⊕ Train 979 crosses the Castle River, a tributary of the Oldman River, east of Cowley, behind C-630M 4505 and SD40 5523 on Thursday, March 26, 1970. *(Bob Loat)*

Above ⊕ At Burmis, mileage 79.1, 4503 leads a short westbound extra on Thursday, August 17, 1972. From Burmis, an ABS signal system is in place for the mountainous section beyond to Crowsnest at mileage 101.1. The CPR installed this stretch of signals to protect the many switching assignments handling the numerous coalmines between Burmis and Coleman. A total of 39 searchlight signals made by General Railway Signal began operating in June 1946. *(Clayton Jones)*

Right ⊕ On Saturday, July 30, 1966, CLC's final (6-1957) H16-44 and that company's last mainline locomotive, 8728, enters the site of the mammoth slide at Frank, mileage 86.4. The slide from Turtle Mountain, to the south of the CPR line, occurred in April 1903, three years after the opening of coalmines in this area of the Crowsnest Pass. A four cubic yard steam shovel in the 400308 to 400310 series stands unused on a short spur. *(Clayton Jones)*

Below ⊕ Train 979 with units 8605, 4425, 4458 and 4080 passes a mini-rodeo west of Blairmore en route to Crowsnest on Sunday, May 31, 1964. Towards the rear of the train, an abandoned right-of-way leads to the site of a Western Canadian Colliery mine where the photographer found an engine-house containing stored 0-6-0 2, ex CPR 6246 and 2-6-0 1 (CLC 5-1914) built for the City of Winnipeg Hydro that is now displayed in Blairmore. *(Bob Sandusky)*

Aldersyde Sub

Above ⊕ The last run of Lethbridge – Vulcan – Calgary Train 311 crosses the Carmangay Bridge over the Little Bow River on Friday, June 2, 1971, with RDC-3 9022 leading RDC-2 9107. The service had begun in April 1955 with the debut of THE CANADIAN. In 1971, THE VULCAN operated return trips on Monday, Wednesday, Friday and Sunday while THE FORT MACLEOD via the subdivision and town of that name ran on the remaining three days of the week. 9022 (Budd 3-1955) was one of five RDC-3's on the CPR and was equipped with 48 seats, a 30' baggage compartment and a Postal section also used for baggage. *(Doug Phillips)*

MacLeod Sub

Above ⊕ On Saturday, November 28, 1970, Train 992 for Fort MacLeod is just getting underway from Alyth Yard and is passing under the CNR overpass a mile south of the Tower at 12th Street East. The overpass, known as McKee on the CNR, formerly the Canadian Northern, allowed access to their downtown passenger terminal at 18th Avenue. Train 992 will follow the Aldersyde Sub from Aldersyde to Coalhurst where traffic will be dropped for points west. *(Doug Phillips)*

Below ⊕ "*The Kingsgate*" was the informal name given to the daily extra en route to the Union Pacific interchange at Kingsgate, B.C. The southbound led by a pair of H16-44's, 8720 and 8609 is approaching the Wilson Coulee, three miles north of Okotoks, mileage 26.3, on Sunday, November 23, 1969. *(Bob Loat)*

Above ◉ Extra 8554 South, *"The Kingsgate"* is seen passing the station at Aldersyde, mileage 31.9, en route to Fort MacLeod on Saturday, January 24, 1970. DFB-15e class F7B 4459 (GMDL 1-1953), now preserved at the West Coast Railway Heritage Park in Squamish, B.C., is in the trailing position. Later, when transporting short wheel-based ore cars from Pine Point in the North West Territories, and running as Train 992 south of Calgary, these trains followed the Aldersyde Sub to avoid damage to the pin-jointed, Single Through Trusses on the multi-span crossing of the Old Man River at Fort MacLeod. Aldersyde was the northern end of the 87-mile Aldersyde Subdivision completed north from Coalhurst to Carmangay in 1910 and to Aldersyde in 1911. *(Doug Phillips)*

Above ◉ At mileage 68, southbound Train 992 is nearing Stavely en route to Fort MacLeod and a connection with North Portal – Eastport, Idaho Train 979. Train 979 in turn forwarded traffic from Chicago – Portal Train 25 on the Soo Line to Union Pacific Train SI-9 for Spokane, Washington. The date is Sunday, February 21, 1971. This 107.3-mile CPR line from the 12th Street East Tower in Calgary to Fort MacLeod opened in 1892, having been constructed, as was the Calgary – Strathcona line to the north under the charter of the Calgary and Edmonton Railway. *(Bob Loat)*

REVELSTOKE DIVISION

Windermere Sub

Above ⊕ Extra 8653 North passes the former flag stop shelter at Edgewater, British Columbia on Saturday, August 24, 1968. The portable station at Edgewater was installed in 1937, 107.1 miles north of Colvalli the junction with the Cranbrook Sub that ran from Crowsnest to Cranbrook in southeastern B.C. The Windermere Sub was completed from Colvalli to Golden on the original Calgary - Vancouver mainline between 1912 and 1914 as the Kootenay Central Railway Co. The "KC" incorporated in 1903 was leased to the CPR in 1911 and amalgamated in 1956. *(Bob Loat)*

Above ⊕ On "Amtrak Day," Saturday, May 1, 1971, H16-44 8718 leads a string of triple hoppers on a southbound extra at the North Switch at Spillimacheen, mileage 125.6. *(Bob Loat)*

Mountain Sub

Above ⊕ The final, standard-gauged steam locomotive built new for a Canadian railway, T1c class Selkirk 5935 (MLW 3-1949) rests on the ready track at Field in July 1952. Specifications of the 2-10-4 included 63" drivers, 25x32" cylinders and a 285 psi boiler generating 76,900 pounds of tractive effort to which a booster added a further 12,500 pounds. This engine was added to the Exporail collection at Saint-Constant, Quebec in May 1963.
(William McChesney, Morning Sun Books Collection)

Above ⊕ Wearing green, CFA16-4 4053 leads GM's 4462, 8668, 4424 and 4061 as they prepare to leave Field for the eastbound assault on the 2.2% grade of Field Hill. It's Sunday afternoon, September 22, 1968. *(Bill Linley)*

Above ⊕ It's 4.05 p.m. Pacific Standard Time on Monday September 14, 1959 at Field, as the late Fred Angus, a CPR computer-specialist, left the comfort of the *Chateau Rouville* on Train 1, THE CANADIAN, to record the meet with Train 8, THE DOMINION. Fred's diary notes that on that day the Soviet spacecraft, Luna II successfully impacted on the Moon. The station, in the International Style, was only six years old, and marked the change from Mountain to Pacific time as well as from the railway's Prairie to Pacific Regions. All locomotive employees running from either Calgary or Revelstoke changed at Field. Passenger train crews serving Field ran through Calgary from Medicine Hat and through Revelstoke from Kamloops. Dining car crews were from Vancouver and sleeping car crews from Winnipeg.
(CRHA Archives, Fond Angus #2363)

Left ⊕ "Travel Treats" brochure of 1954.
(Gerry Gaugl Collection)

Above ⊕ Second 85, behind a trio of Train Masters, ducks under the Trans-Canada Highway just west of Field on Sunday May 19, 1963. 8905 is the only preserved Train Master and resides at Exporail in Saint-Constant, Quebec. Dominating the background is 10,496-foot Mount Stephen that was named in 1886 after George Stephen, who became the CPR's first president in 1881. *(Peter Cox)*

Left ⊕ The bridge over Ottertail Creek feels the weight of Extra 4029 East as it ascends the Kicking Horse Valley en route to Field, some six miles away on Sunday, April 14, 1963. The Kicking Horse River in Yoho National Park is a major headwater of the Columbia River.
(Peter Cox)

Left Center ⊕ Although shorn of its sleepers and diner, Train 8, THE DOMINION, still has a sizeable consist of mail, express and coaches as it arrives at Golden, mileage 35.0, around 2.00 p.m. on a day in May 1964. The three piggyback flats carrying CP Merchandise Services shipments were included in the consist departing Vancouver at 8.00 p.m. the previous evening and are destined for Winnipeg. All mail and express service on THE DOMINION would end on June 24, 1964. CPR rails were extended from Laggan, North West Territories, latterly Lake Louise, Alberta, through Field to Beavermouth, mileage 63.0 in 1884.
(Doug Phillips)

Below ⊕ Photographer Peter Cox watches as DRS-16j class H16-44 8728 switches in front of the Golden station that opened in 1904, on Sunday morning, September 2, 1962. As this train is originating in Golden, it is not governed by the 19Y setting on the order board for a passing mainline train. Golden is the northern terminal of the Windermere Sub, and became a much busier junction with the advent of unit-train shipments of Vancouver-bound metallurgical export coal from the East Kootenay Coalfields around Fernie in the late 1960's.
(Keith Anderson)

Train 2 occupies the full 585 feet of Mountain Creek Bridge at mileage 70.8, as constructed in 1902 replacing an original wooden trestle. FP9 1412 leads the train on Labor Day Monday, September 3, 1962. Mount McNicoll, named for former CPR Vice-President David McNicoll (1852-1916), towers to 11,351 feet in the background.
(Peter Cox)

Above ⊕ At mileage 76.3, Extra 4080 East descends the 2.25% grade of Beaver Hill and crosses the Stoney Creek Bridge, as strengthened in 1929, on Saturday, April 17, 1965. Stoney Creek rises on the Hermit Glacier on the shoulder of Mount Shaughnessy and falls to the Beaver River in the trough of the eastern approach to Rogers Pass. *(Peter Cox)*

Right ⊕ Images of the Stoney Creek Bridge by celebrated company photographer Nicholas Morant were a favorite for timetables and travel guides including this one from 1963. *(Bill Linley Collection)*

Below ⊕ On Sunday, May 19, 1968, Field – Coquitlam Train 67 led by 8825, 8677, 8671, 8601 and 8525 hammers its way to the eastern portal of the five-mile, concrete-lined Connaught Tunnel of 1916. Its length was not exceeded in North America until Great Northern's 7.8-mile Cascade Tunnel of 1929. Originally double-tracked, it was singled in 1958 to allow for easier transit of piggyback cars and dimensional traffic. The tunnel cut 4.3 route miles off the final section of the CPR mainline as completed from Beavermouth to Savona in 1885. *(Doug Wingfield)*

WESTWARD
ACROSS CANADA
BY *Canadian Pacific*

"The Canadian"   "The Dominion"
CANADA'S SCENIC DOME ROUTE

Left ◉ Mid-train helpers SD40s 5540, 5542 and 5529 assist 8825 on the climb from Beavermouth to Glacier. They will be cut off at Glacier and return to Beavermouth for the next push. *(Doug Wingfield)*

Above ◉ Train 7, THE DOMINION, has crested the 3,787-foot summit of Rogers Pass and emerges from the Connaught Tunnel under 9,459-foot Mount Macdonald approaching mileage 85.5 at Glacier at 3.38 p.m. on Canadian Thanksgiving Day, Monday, October 12, 1964. Mount Macdonald was named for Sir John A. Macdonald, a Conservative who was Canada's first Prime Minister in 1867. The structure in the background includes two large fans that push air through the tunnel to void it of noxious gases. A further run of 40.2 miles down the Illicilliwaet River from Glacier will bring THE DOMINION to the division point of Revelstoke. *(Keith Anderson)*

Right ◉ GP9 8678 works with a tie-gang on the backtrack at Glacier on Wednesday, July 16, 1969. Opened in 1917, the log-style station is located in the heart of the Selkirk Mountains and Glacier National Park. *(Clayton Jones)*

Above ◉ Train 5, the Expo Limited, pauses at Revelstoke for a 45-minute servicing and crew change after 5.05 p.m. on Monday, July 3, 1967. Each trainset featured a Winnipeg – Vancouver *Skyline* dome-coach and a Montreal – Vancouver *Park* series dome-observation car. At the rear of the train are large blocks of ice waiting to replenish the ice-activated air conditioning systems of the vintage diner and heavyweight sleepers. With a few exceptions, this will be their last season of operation. Ahead lies the climb to Clanwilliam, and beyond Sicamous, a further climb over Notch Hill en route to a 6.30 a.m. arrival in Vancouver.

(Bob Webster, Bill Linley Collection)

Shuswap Sub

Left ◉ The "Seeing Canada" brochure provided a complete list of stations and scenic highlights while advising photographers to use a CC30R for color film to correct for the green-tinted dome windows.

(Gerry Gaugl Collection)

Below ◉ DPA-15d class FP7 1432 brings Train 2, The Canadian, across the Columbia at 7.15 a.m. on Sunday, May 19, 1963. The first three passenger cars are U class fourteen-section tourist sleepers, part of a group of twenty-two 85-ton cars built between 1921 and 1926 and upgraded in 1954 with mechanical air-conditioning and stainless steel cladding to match The Canadian's new Budd equipment. Tourist class featured coach fares with a small premium for berth space without the need for a first class fare. For example, in The Canadian's inaugural summer of 1955, a tourist lower berth from Toronto to Lake Louise was $83.15 versus $105.55 for a lower in a Budd-built sleeper. It was intended that meals would be enjoyed in the *Skyline* mid-train dome. *(Peter Cox)*

Above ⊕ Leaving Revelstoke, the Columbia River is crossed on this 1,122-foot bridge by a fifty-one car westbound led by FP7 4034 on Sunday, April 18, 1965. This bridge replaced an earlier crossing in 1907 and was similarly replaced in 1968. *(Clayton Jones)*

Below ⊕ SD40's 5552 5554 5527 and 5534 bring an eastbound through the snowsheds along Three Valley Lake, mileage 13.5, on Thursday, September 12, 1968, and will soon begin the 1.4% descent to the Columbia River crossing. *(Bill Linley)*

Left ⊕ At 9.00 a.m. on Victoria Day, Monday, May 20, 1963, Train 8, THE DOMINION, is about to duck under the Trans-Canada Highway just west of Craigellachie, mileage 28.0 of the Shuswap Sub. Craigellachie was named after a high crag in Morayshire, Scotland where a beacon fire summoned the Clan Grant in time of battle. "Stand Fast Craigellachie" was the battle cry of the Grants and was the message transmitted from London in 1884, by CPR President, George Stephen, to his cousin and CPR director, Donald Smith in Montreal, on the successful negotiation of a loan pivotal to the completion of the transcontinental line. A cairn marks the Last Spike driven by Donald Smith in the CPR's line to the Pacific Ocean on November 7, 1885. Construction in 1885 completed the line from Beavermouth on the Mountain Sub to the east, and from Savona on the Thompson Sub to the west, a distance of 216 miles. *(Peter Cox)*

Above ⊕ At 8.15 on a July evening in 1952, five month old DPA-15b class FP7 4059 leading Train 7, THE DOMINION, pauses beside the combination station-hotel at Sicamous, mileage 44.2. 4059 was renumbered and regeared to 1417 in January 1955 for the advent of THE CANADIAN and was retired following a turntable-pit fire at the Drake Street roundhouse in Vancouver in 1971. The Hotel Sicamous, leased from the CPR, was a large wooden structure dating to 1899. Perched on the lakeside, the hotel operated until 1956 and offered travelers a way to schedule daylight trips from hotel to hotel across the mountains or to conveniently await the daily-except-Sunday mixed train to Kelowna in the Okanagan Valley to the south.
(William J. McChesney, Morning Sun Books Collection)

Above ⊕ During his visit in July, 1952, Bill McChesney walked west along the shore of Shuswap Lake at Sicamous to record this scene of P2k class 2-8-2 5462 with a westbound freight. The oil-burning Mikado was delivered in September 1948 from MLW as the first of the final dozen 2-8-2's purchased by the CPR. The first eight engines were assigned to Revelstoke in December 1952, and sister 5468 is displayed inside the Revelstoke Railway Museum. The engines developed 57,500 lbs of tractive effort from a 275 psi boiler equipped with 22x32" cylinders and rode on 63" drivers.
(Morning Sun Books Collection)

Above ⊕ As seen from the rear car of the eastbound DOMINION on Tuesday, December 22, 1964, GP9 8672 is holding in the siding with the eastbound Kamloops – Revelstoke wayfreight. The station opened in 1964 replacing the former hotel/station.
(Keith Anderson)

Right ⊕ Having run around a freight derailment involving miscommunication with a mid-train robot unit, westbound GP9 8690 is leaving the 162-car siding at Canoe, mileage 57.1, on the southern shore of Shuswap Lake. The date is Thursday, September 12, 1968, however, the station dates from 1909. *(Bill Linley)*

Below ⊕ A trio of SD40s brings a westbound over the east siding switch at Salmon Arm in August 1967. General Railway Signal provided the signal equipment for the ABS installation between Taft, mileage 23.9, and this location just east of mileage 63.2 in 1951. The following year, ABS signalling was installed between Salmon Arm and Kamloops, completing the program to install signals between Calgary and Vancouver that had begun in the 1920s. To handle increasing traffic the CPR began converting the ABS to Centralized Traffic Control with the first portion between Revelstoke and Taft completed in 1959. CTC came to the 80.4-mile Taft – Pritchard portion of the Shuswap Subdivision in 1968. The remaining twenty-four miles to Kamloops were double-tracked in 1914. *(Stan Smaill)*

Above ⊕ The EXPO LIMITED, Train 6, sparkles in the early morning sun as it passes the station at Notch Hill, mileage 79.5, on a Holiday Monday, July 3, 1967. Lead DRS-17b class GP9 8526 (GMDL 8-1955) is one of several units equipped with a fabricated pilot in place of the normal footboards. It may have been hastily installed, as most such pilots featured black and yellow safety stripes. A 1.7-mile siding at this point was equipped with 20 mph spring switches directing traffic to the right and frequently easing the setting of retainers at the top of the descending 19.1-mile, 1.6% eastbound grade to Tappen.

(Bob Webster, Bill Linley Collection)

Above ⊕ S1a 2-10-2 5805 departs Kamloops for the 128.3-mile run over the Shuswap Sub to its home terminal of Revelstoke with an eastbound extra on Dominion Day, Wednesday, July 1, 1953. *(Stan Styles, Keith Anderson Collection)*

Okanagan Sub

Above ⊕ Except Sunday mixed Train 708 had departed Sicamous at 10.10 a.m. in July, 1952 and is running along the Sicamous Narrows as it begins the 79.7 mile run to Kelowna on Lake Okanagan. The last 33.5 miles of the trip beyond Vernon would traverse the CNR's Kamloops – Kelowna route that opened in 1925. D10j 962 (MLW 9-1912) displays the maroon tender panel and striping uniquely retained on this Ten-wheeler following its application for its turn on a system-wide 1947 tour by CPR president W. M. Neal. *(William McChesney, Morning Sun Books Collection)*

Below ⊕ Using the charter of the Shuswap & Okanagan, the CPR completed a 51-mile route from Sicamous to Okanagan Landing, 4.8 miles south of Vernon, mileage 46.2 in 1891. Freight and passenger service was introduced with steamboats on a 104-mile route along Okanagan Lake to Penticton. Passenger service ended in 1936 but freight service continued to serve lakefront communities between Kelowna and Penticton until 1972. The steam tug *Naramata*, fabricated at the Port Arthur (Ontario) Shipyard in 1913, and now preserved at Okanagan Landing is seen near the CPR's barge at Kelowna on Friday, April 22, 1966. *(Bill Linley Collection)*

Above ⊕ October 25, 1959 schedule for chartered bus service to the Okanagan. *(Gerry Gaugl Collection)*

Osoyoos Sub

Above ⊕ At mileage 10.1, on Thursday morning, June 20, 1963, H16-44 8603 brings a southbound extra across the 496' long pile trestle over Skaha Lake. Opened in stages beginning in 1923, the final 10.3-mile section of the Osoyoos Sub south of Haynes opened in 1944, the CPR's last new construction in British Columbia prior to the coal-driven expansion decades later. *(John Rushton)*

Below ⊕ In the twilight of fresh fruit shipments over the 36.4-mile Osoyoos Sub, Work Extra 8605 is northbound passing the MacLean & Fitzpatrick orchard just north of the end of track at Osoyoos near the Washington State border on Saturday, August 3, 1968. Osoyoos Lake is in the background. *(Bob Loat)*

CANYON DIVISION

Thompson Sub

Above ⊕ P2b class Mikado 5314 (MLW 1-1921) is lifting a westbound extra out of the Kamloops yard in September 1954. The Kamloops-assigned coal-burner was equipped with 63" drivers, 23.5x32" cylinders and a 200 psi boiler generating 56,100 pounds of tractive effort. In 1948, the 1907 station was extensively remodeled in the Moderne style. *(Stan Styles, Keith Anderson Collection)*

Right ⊕ While serving as the rear flagman on CNR Train 9, THE PANORAMA, Peter Cox was alert to a "running meet" albeit on parallel railways with CPR Extra 4076 East at Basque, mileage 55.9. The meet happened around 12.30 p.m. on Tuesday, March 23, 1965. In 1884, construction of the Thompson Sub proceeded from the western terminus at North Bend, mileage 121.5 for 96.3 miles to Savona on the southern shore of Kamloops Lake. *(Peter Cox)*

Right ⊕ "Front to rear," SD40 5533 leads a westbound extra at mileage 87, 7.9 miles east of Lytton, with its van visible to the left of the cab. On the far side of the Thompson River Canyon, beyond the Trans-Canada Highway, the entire consist of an eastbound CNR wayfreight trailing a combine is visible at Pitquah as it proceeds along the Ashcroft Sub from Boston Bar to Kamloops on Tuesday, September 22, 1970. *(Peter Cox)*

Princeton Sub

Above ⊕ On Monday evening, Labor Day, September 3, 1962, RDC-3 9022 and RDC-2 9107 are at Penticton. The station opened in 1941 in a mock-Tudor style. Daily Train 46 had arrived at 8.00 a.m. with *Dayliner* 9022 having departed Spences Bridge, mileage 72.8 of the Thompson Sub at 2.50 a.m. following a connection with Train 4 from Vancouver. *Dayliner* 9107 had arrived from Nelson at 5.25 p.m. as Train 45 and would depart at 6.30 p.m. to make a five minute connection at Spences Bridge with THE DOMINION, at 11.50 p.m. for a 7.00 a.m. arrival in Vancouver. 9022 would leave on the 8¼-hour trip to Nelson as Train 46 at 8.50 on Tuesday. The Nelson – Penticton service was repeated on Thursday and Friday while the Nelson – Medicine Hat service was also daily. After 1958, an overnight stay was required in Nelson for through Vancouver – Medicine Hat passengers on this route following threats to the safe passage of trains by the Doukhobors, a militant religious sect. *(Keith Anderson)*

Right ⊕ In June 1971, an eastbound 'Princeton Turn' roars past mileage 64.0 of the Princeton Sub as it winds its way through the Belfort Loops about two-thirds of the way up the 'Jura Hill'. GP9's 8836 and 8649 will be at full throttle for most of the ten-mile ascent from Princeton to Jura as the train heads back home to Penticton. *(Joe Smuin)*

Below ⊕ Extra 8814 East leads GP9 8664 near mile 66 of the Princeton Sub about four miles east of Princeton on Tuesday afternoon, July 30, 1968. The Geeps are climbing the notorious 'Jura Hill' where pushers were required in steam days. The driving of the last spike on the Kettle Valley Railway at Princeton in April 1915 completed a through Canadian rail route across Southern British Columbia. *(Bob Loat)*

Above ⊕ Penticton-assigned oil burning N2b class Consolidation 3734 (MLW 11-1912) is switching log cars at Brookmere on Tuesday, September 18, 1951. The 2-8-0 had 63" drivers, 23x32 cylinders, and a 190-psi boiler that produced 43,400 lbs of tractive effort. Prior to the abandonment of the Coquihalla Sub in 1961, Brookmere, mileage 108.6, was a division point between the Princeton Sub to Penticton in the east and the 56.6-mile Coquihalla Sub to Odlum on the Cascade Sub 88 miles east of Vancouver. *(R. S. Ritchie)*

Left ⊕ After the devastating washouts of November 1959, Penticton – Vancouver trains were rerouted via Spences Bridge and the Merritt Sub that connected with the former Coquihalla line at Brodie, 4.3 miles west of Brookmere. In 1962, with the closure of the Kettle Valley Division headquartered in Penticton, the Princeton Sub was extended to include the former Merritt Sub. Brookmere closed as a home terminal for crews in 1966. DRS-17f class GP9 8831 pilots an extra east at Brookmere on Saturday, August 10, 1968. The enclosed water tank held 48,000 U.S. gallons. *(Bob Webster, Bill Linley Collection)*

Below ⊕ Extra 8551 West pulls past the 1909 station at Merritt, mileage 138.1, on Thursday, May 28, 1970. When opened by the CPR under the charter of the Nicola, Kamloops & Similkameen Coal & Railway Co. in 1907, the 39.7-mile line from Spences Bridge to Merritt continued for 7.3 miles to the coalfields at Nicola. Following construction from Merritt to Brodie in 1910, the Merritt-Nicola portion of the line became a spur when the line was transferred to Kettle Valley Railway administration in late 1915. *(Clayton Jones)*

Mission Sub

Above ⊕ Although boiler-equipped prior to 1955, DRS-4-4-1000 8004 (Baldwin 12-1948) would not have needed this feature at 2.00 p.m. on a warm Tuesday, June 30, 1959. Mixed Train 809 is about to make its last run back to Vancouver from Huntingdon, the southern end of the 10.1-mile branch from Mission City, mileage 87.3 of the Cascade Sub. Serving the fertile agricultural lands of the Fraser River Valley, the Mission Sub opened in 1891 providing direct interchange at the Huntingdon - Sumas, Washington border crossing with the Milwaukee Road from Bellingham and the Northern Pacific from Seattle. *(Keith Anderson)*

Cascade Sub

Right ⊕ Vancouver-based G3g Pacific 2387 (CLC 5-1942) pauses for scheduled servicing at the division point of North Bend at 2.30 p.m. on a July day in 1952. Train 2, the transcontinental local, will arrive in Montreal on the fifth morning out of Vancouver. Construction of the mainline from Mission, mileage 87.3 to North Bend was completed in 1884.
(William McChesney, Morning Sun Books Collection)

Below ⊕ Extra 4034 East is east of Choate, mileage 35.6 in the Fraser River Canyon, with F7B 4448 and GP9's 8640 and 8676 on Victoria Day, Monday, May 21, 1962. *(Keith Anderson)*

Left ⊕ Opposite Hope, Extra 8632 West meets an eastbound powered by FP7 4040 at Haig, mileage 40.1 on May 21, 1962. By 1968, the installation of CTC removed Haig from the timetable and replaced it with a 150-car passing track at Katz, mileage 44.9. Until on-line washouts on the Coquihalla Sub near Lear in November 1959, Odlum at mileage 41.6 was the junction switch for the line to Brookmere and beyond across Southern British Columbia to the Crowsnest Pass. *(Keith Anderson)*

Below ⊕ An eastbound test train includes dynamometer car 62 at Kanaka Creek, mileage 101.5 on the 56.7-mile stretch of ABS equipped double track from Pitt River to Ruby Creek on Thursday, September 28, 1966. This was the first SD40-powered train to depart Coquitlam Yard.

(Peter Cox, Bill Linley Collection)

VANCOUVER DIVISION

Cascade Sub

Above ⊕ DRS-10a 8008 (Baldwin 12-1948) exits the west end of the Pitt River Bridge and is about to enter Coquitlam Yard on Monday, October 22, 1962. CPR's initial dieselization study of the Esquimalt and Nanaimo's operation on Vancouver Island would most probably have recommended the 1000 hp Alco RS-1 as MLW was the CPR's preferred diesel supplier in the 1940's. MLW was unable to arrange timely delivery, so CLC secured the business and contracted Baldwin in Eddystone, Pennsylvania to build thirteen DRS-4-4-1000's that were similar to the RS-1. *(Peter Cox)*

Above ⊕ S-4's 7107 and 7100 exit the Coquitlam River Bridge and pass the 1893-era station at Coquitlam, mileage 112.5 on Sunday, May 8, 1960. The ten S-4's of class DS-10k, 7099 – 7108, were built about a year prior to the introduction of the model in the U.S. by Alco. These two units were included in the five units originally assigned to Montreal and were equipped with MU for transfer service in 1951. *(Keith Anderson)*

Above ⊕ FP7 4040 treads carefully on a shoofly around a new underpass at the east end of Coquitlam Yard in September 1962. The 4040 was renumbered 1433 and equipped with 89 mph trucks in April 1955 along with the 4039 (1434) to allow a highspeed connection of Edmonton – Calgary Train 528, THE STAMPEDER, with the eastbound CANADIAN. Changing service requirements saw them revert to 65 mph gearing and their former numbers in May 1960.
(Max Tschumi, Bill Linley Collection)

Left ⊕ On Thursday, March 6, 1969, GP9 8689 leads an eastbound train of empty 70-ton coal hoppers at Port Moody, the original western terminus of the CPR. The station opened in 1908 and was moved a half mile east to mileage 116.1 in early 1945. *(Peter Cox)*

Left ⊕ As seen from the Second Narrows Bridge, Baldwin 8005 powers a westbound on Saturday, June 11, 1960. *(Keith Anderson)*

Above ⊕ On Saturday, April 22, 1967, GP9 8812 is passing below the construction site for the new railway crossing of the Second Narrows of Burrard Inlet. Owned by the CNR, it features a vertical lift-span on a route that opened in 1968 to provide direct access for the CNR and CPR to the Pacific Great Eastern and North Shore industries via the Great Northern connection from their Westminster Sub. *(Keith Anderson)*

Right ⊕ S-4 7112 brings a cut of cars through the bascule bridge crossing of the Second Narrows onto the Cascade Sub in June 1961. The low-level crossing opened in 1927 and accommodated both trains and automobiles. Above towers the new automobile-carrying Second Narrows Bridge that opened in 1960, replacing the initial replacement that collapsed on June 17, 1958 with the loss of 19 lives. *(Keith Anderson)*

Right ⊕ Train 46 with RDC-2 9198 is outbound for Penticton just after 8.00 a.m. on Tuesday, February 23, 1960. It was due into Penticton via Spences Bridge at 3.05 p.m. However, the circuitous routing via Spences Bridge due to the closure of the Coquihalla Sub would result in arrival around 6.00 p.m. A second *Dayliner* would depart Penticton at 3.30 p.m. as Train 47 for Vancouver with a scheduled arrival at 10.40 p.m., but a likely arrival of 2.00 a.m. having met the eastbound at Osprey Lake on the Princeton Sub. The *Dayliner* is nearing Second Narrows, mileage 124.1, and is about to pass the siding switch leading to the grounds of the Pacific National Exhibition. The line to what would become downtown Vancouver opened in 1887 in a relocation of the CPR's western terminus from Port Moody. The line was double-tracked in 1912.
(Keith Anderson)

Right ⊕ As seen from the Commissioner Street Bridge with the Alberta Wheel Pools Terminal in the background, DS-4-4-1000 (Baldwin 10-1948) DS-10g class switcher 7073 and sister unit 7072 run along the shores of Burrard Inlet on Friday, June 5, 1964. These units received MU control in January 1958. Between 1957 and 1968 the two-dozen Baldwins had been similarly equipped and remained assigned to Vancouver. *(John Rushton)*

Above ⊕ D10g 922 is seen from the pedestrian walkway to the CPR Marine terminal in July 1952. As we have seen, 922 migrated to the Prairies and served at Bredenbury, Saskatchewan in 1959 prior to its scrapping in January, 1960. Out of sight to the right is the north portal of the tunnel leading to the Drake Street roundhouse and yards.
(William McChesney, Morning Sun Books Collection)

Left ⊕ CP's first Baldwin diesel (3-1948) and sole occupant of class DS-10f poses at the N-yard engine facility adjacent to the Marine Terminal on the Vancouver waterfront in 1948. A builder's photograph shows the unit in black with yellow lettering; however, it was soon repainted to this scheme as applied to the final ten DS-4-4-1000's that followed later in 1948. A comparison in early 1948 between the 7065 and Alco S-2 7033 in Montreal revealed that the Baldwin was less fuel-efficient. Neither the Baldwin switcher nor road switcher generated a repeat order. MLW remained the predominant supplier of switchers to the CPR. A diesel maintainer based in the shed to the left kept the units in service from shift to shift. *(Andrew Cassidy Collection)*

Above ⊕ Last hurrah! On Wednesday, September 1, 1965, THE DOMINION is living on borrowed time. By January, 1966 it would be gone and early evening scenes such as this view of adjacent *Park* cars on transcontinental passenger trains would vanish save for a brief reprieve accorded by the departures of the EXPO LIMITED during Canada's Centennial Year, 1967. *(Max Tschumi, Bill Linley Collection)*

Above ⊕ RDC-2's 9197 and 9196 are about to depart for Penticton as Train 46 at 8.00 a.m. on Friday, July 10, 1959. Behind the train is a portion of the CPR's Vancouver station that opened in 1914, following the designs of the Montreal firm of Barrott, Blackader and Webster. *(Keith Anderson)*

Above ⊕ The 5,251-ton *Princess Joan* of the CPR's British Columbia Coast Service awaits passengers for her morning run to Victoria in July 1952. Her usual berth, Pier D was destroyed in a fire in 1937 and operations for both the Coast Service and the Trans-Pacific *Empress* liners were based at the newer Pier B-C that had opened on July 4, 1927. The *Princess Joan* was built in 1930 at the Fairfield yard in Govan, Scotland that had built many vessels for the CPR. At this time, her normal run was the overnight service from Victoria together with a daytime return voyage running opposite her sister ship, the *Princess Elizabeth*. The two ships featured many staterooms and could accommodate 405 first class and 26 second class passengers along with 48 automobiles. Both ships were laid up in 1959 and were sold in 1960 to the Epirotiki Line becoming the *Hermes* (*Princess Joan*) and *Pegasus* for a further decade of service in the Mediterranean.
(William McChesney, Morning Sun Books Collection)

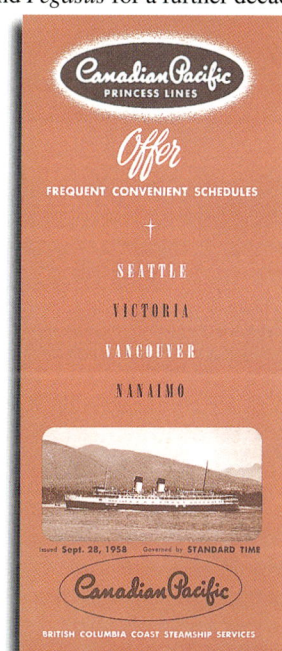

Above ⊕ British Columbia Coast Steamship Services schedule, September 1958.
(Gerry Gaugl Collection)

Above ⊕ G4a Pacific 2709 (Angus 3-1920) rides the 90' turntable at the 22-stall Drake Street roundhouse of 1911. The 4-6-2 featured 70" drivers, 24.5x30" cylinders, a 200 psi boiler and 43,700 pounds of tractive effort. Several of the 18 engines of this class were oil-burners assigned to passenger service between Kamloops and Vancouver beyond the Western reaches of the Selkirks. Located along False Creek, Drake Street was accessed by a tunnel built in 1932 from the west end of the Vancouver terminal and serviced passenger power and switchers. The last survivor of its class, 2709 served as a temporary replacement for the steam plant at the Drake Street roundhouse until January, 1962 when it gained notoriety as the only CPR steamer scrapped in Vancouver. *(Keith Anderson)*

Westminster Sub

Right ⊕ As seen from the railway bridge that Canadian National, Great Northern and B.C. Electric used to access New Westminster from the south bank of the Fraser River, on Friday, December 18, 1964, GP9 8484 pulls an eastbound cut of cars along the north bank of the Fraser River in New Westminster. The 8.4-mile line opened from Coquitlam in 1887. The track to the left is a Great Northern line to the New Westminster waterfront.
(Peter Cox)

E & N DIVISION

Victoria Sub

Above ⊕ North of downtown Victoria, DS-10g class Baldwin DS4-4-1000 7074 moves north along Store Street to service local industries on Tuesday, July 25, 1967. Rails reached British Columbia's capital from the north in 1894, following completion of the original mainline from Wellington to Esquimalt by the Esquimalt & Nanaimo Railway Co. in 1887. The E&N came under control of the CPR in 1905 and was leased by them in 1912. *(Bob Loat)*

Right ⊕ "Dayliner" schedule for Vancouver Island *(Gerry Gaugl Collection)*

Below ⊕ Baldwins 8008 and 8007 approach Ladysmith, mileage 58.4, with a northbound extra on Monday, June 29, 1970. The log booming operation of Crown Zellerbach is in the background with Thetis and Cooper Islands in the distance. The 18-mile Lake Cowichan branch diverged at Hayward, mileage 41.6, to access the operations of the Pacific Logging Company. *(Bob Wilt, Ken McCutcheon Collection)*

Above ⊕ On Thursday, May 23, 1968, 8009 is north of Ladysmith with a southbound load of interchanged MacMillan Bloedel logs bound for their log dump at Chemainus. *(Peter Cox)*

Above ⊕ North of Ladysmith, the CPR crossed and interchanged with the Comox Logging and Railway Company and MacMillan Bloedel. A pair of Baldwins is southbound in May 1969, while MacMillan Bloedel 2-8-2 saddletank number 1055 waits at the tank prior to returning to the woods in the Nanaimo River Valley. Currently operating on the Alberni Pacific Railway in Port Alberni, Baldwin built the logging engine in May of 1929. *(Stan Smaill)*

Above ⊕ More than 50% of CPR's small fleet of Baldwin road switchers is visible in this view at Wellcox on Thursday afternoon, October 16, 1969. The thirteen units had arrived in 1949 and quickly achieved Canada's first complete dieselization of a railway operating division. Wellcox, on a spur off the mainline at Stockett, mileage 70, two point five miles south of Nanaimo was opened in 1955 on lands formerly occupied by the Canadian Colleries (Dunsmuir) Limited and replaced the division point of Wellington, 4.8 miles north of Nanaimo. A new ferry slip and diesel maintenance facilities were included in the yard at Wellcox. *(John M. Robinson, Glenn Williams Collection)*

Above ⊕ The *Princess of Nanaimo* is alongside the 1950-era terminal in Nanaimo on Saturday, June 20, 1953. She was built in 1949 by the Fairfield Company in Govan and entered service between Vancouver and Nanaimo on Vancouver Island on Wednesday, June 27, 1951, supplementing the 1928 vintage *Princess Elaine*. The 6,787-ton steam-turbine ship could be side-loaded with up to 150 automobiles on two decks while accommodating up to 1500-day passengers. Due to the ship's short yet wide construction, locals nicknamed her 'The Blimp'. In the face of strong competition from the provincially owned B.C. Ferries, she was transferred in 1963 to the CPR's Bay of Fundy service as the *Princess of Acadia* running between Saint John, New Brunswick and Digby, Nova Scotia. *(Omer Lavallee, Collection of R. S. Ritchie)*

Above ⊕ RDC-1 9055 on Train 2 soars over the Englishman's River at mileage 93, south of Parkesville at 2.40 p.m. on Friday, July 28, 1967. Parkesville was the junction point for the 38.8-mile Port Alberni Sub that crossed the forestry rich island to reach Port Alberni on the Pacific Ocean. This branch brought total mileage on Vancouver Island to 196.5. *(Bob Loat)*

Left ⊕ E & N Timetable 1951 *(Gerry Gaugl Collection)*

Below ⊕ A twenty-minute layover was afforded at Courtenay between the arrival of Train 1 and the 1.30 p.m. departure of Train 2 for Victoria. RDC-3 9024 awaits departure time on Thursday, March 4, 1965. The southbound run consumed four hours following the introduction of *Dayliners* in 1955. Previously the conventional trains hauled by one of the first five Baldwins that were steam generator equipped required almost 6 ½ hours. Rails reached the end of track at Courtenay, mileage 139.7 in 1914 and provided an end-on connection with Headquarters operation of the Comox Logging and Railway. *(Keith Anderson)*

KOOTENAY DIVISION

Cranbrook Sub

Above ⊕ The CPR, using the charter of the British Columbia Southern, laid rails west from the Alberta – B.C. border at Crowsnest to Kootenay Landing on Kootenay Lake, west of Cranbrook, in 1898. At mileage 18.2 of the Cranbrook Sub, Michel was an important coal mining and preparation area. H16-44 8608 switches loads at Crow's Nest Pass Coal's coking plant at Michel on Friday, September 20, 1968. The coke was used in base metal refining in Southern B.C. and in the Pacific Northwest. *(Bill Linley)*

Above ⊕ FP7 4061 and CPB16-4 4471 are eastbound passing the 1910-era station at Natal, mileage 14.6, with 116 coal empties on Easter Sunday, April 14, 1968. The train is returning to the mines at Coleman, Alberta on the Crowsnest Sub and is an early example of unit-train operation on the CPR. *(Bob Loat)*

Left ⊕ Train 74 heads through Wardner, mileage 77.1, around 2.00 p.m. on Tuesday, June 28, 1966. On that day, this daily train was ordered out of Cranbrook around 11.00 a.m. over the 27.7 miles to Colvalli and thence north on the Windermere Sub to Golden. This portion of the Cranbrook Sub would be abandoned in 1971 due to the construction of the Libby Dam in Montana. A new, ten-mile direct line to Cranbrook opened in 1970 from Fort Steele, 23 miles north of Colvalli on the Windermere Sub. *(John Rushton)*

Kimberley Sub

Left ◉ Daily except Sunday Number 79 out of Cranbrook is arriving at Chapman Camp, mileage 16.3, on Friday morning, July 8, 1966 behind CLC's 8711 and 8914. The 18.7-mile Kimberley Sub was built by the CPR under the charter of the British Columbia Southern Railway Co. and opened in 1900 to serve the Sullivan lead-zinc mine that was subsequently owned by Cominco, a CPR subsidiary. The ore concentrated at Chapman Camp was shipped to the Cominco smelter at Tadanac. A large, ancillary fertilizer plant was located just south of Chapman Camp. *(John Rushton)*

Kingsgate Sub

Above ◉ SD40 5523 and C-630M 4505 have recently arrived at Eastport, Idaho with Train 979 on Good Friday, March 27, 1970. Train 979 operated from North Portal via Lethbridge and could have included through traffic that had left Chicago at 9.00 p.m. the previous Sunday evening on Soo Line Train 3.
(Bob Loat)

Left ◉ A trio of GP9s including 8677, 8649 and 8679 passes UP GP9 161 (EMD 3-1954) at Eastport, Idaho on Tuesday morning, August 31, 1971. They had just turned on the wye after bringing Train 979 from Cranbrook over the 10.5 miles of the Kingsgate Sub from Yahk. The Kingsgate Sub opened in 1906 to provide a cross border connection to Spokane over the 140-mile Spokane International. The SI was acquired by the Union Pacific in 1958 and operated as its Spokane Sub within the Oregon Division. The UP units will soon depart on Train SI-9 for Spokane, Washington. *(Bill Linley)*

Nelson Sub

Above ⊕ Medicine Hat assigned G3g Pacific 2381 awaits the 2.45 p.m. departure of Train 11 at Cranbrook on Monday, June 15, 1951. Train 11 left Medicine Hat daily at 5.00 a.m. with a through 12-1 (12 section, one drawing room) Regina – Vancouver sleeper, connecting from Train 7 THE DOMINION, to arrive on the Pacific Coast at 5.25 p.m. the second day. Meal service was provided in a buffet-parlor car. The reconstruction of the station in 1945 introduced the International Style including the non-traditional colors of cream yellow and pea green.
(Omer Lavallee, R. S. Ritchie Collection)

Above ⊕ CPA16-4 4057 leads an Extra West toward Nelson across the Moyie River, Peavine Creek and along the shores of Moyie Lake on the Victoria Day Holiday, Monday, May 23, 1966. The Jerome Tunnel lies just ahead at mileage 14. *(Keith Anderson)*

Above ⊕ All was quiet at Yahk, mileage 40.6, on Wednesday morning, June 19, 1968 except for the idling of 8555 in a back track, until Train #984 with 4052 and 4056 arrived with the overnight freight from Nelson. Shortly after the arrival of #984, Train 980 with 8722, 4454 and 4030 arrived from the UP connection at Kingsgate. In a few minutes, a westbound extra from Cranbrook with 8726 and 8556 will arrive and pick up 8555 before clearing in the yard allowing Train 984 to depart for Cranbrook. Train 980 will follow and lift cars from Train 984 in Cranbrook as it continues its journey towards Lethbridge, Moose Jaw and ultimately, the Soo Line connection at North Portal. The station dates from 1912. *(Clayton Jones)*

Above ⊕ An Extra West from Cranbrook with units 8722, 8548, 4435 and 8716 is arriving at Nelson, mileage 137.8, on the West Arm of Kootenay Lake on the afternoon of Friday, May 31, 1968. The Highway 3A bridge is in the background. Lake steamers and car floats provided service from Kootenay Landing, mileage 83 to Proctor 20.3 miles east of Nelson, from 1902 until 1930, when rails were installed along the west shore of Kootenay Lake to complete a continuous rail route from across Southern B.C. *(John Rushton)*

Boundary Sub

Above ⊕ The Nelson Shop opened in 1953 to maintain the CLC diesels as well as the small number of GMD's and MLW's assigned to the Kootenays. The shop specialized in the CLC units and continued in operation until the last of the Company's 69 CLC road units were retired in 1975. Late in the evening of Tuesday, September 17, 1968, 4104 and 8711 await their next assignment. *(Bill Linley)*

Right ⊕ West of Thrums, mileage 19.9, Train 81 behind 4056, 4449, 8713 and 8555 drums alongside the Kootenay River on its way across the Boundary Sub from Nelson to Midway, mileage 126.6, on September 18, 1968. *(Bill Linley)*

Right ⊕ CLC handbook from February 1956.
(Bill Linley Collection)

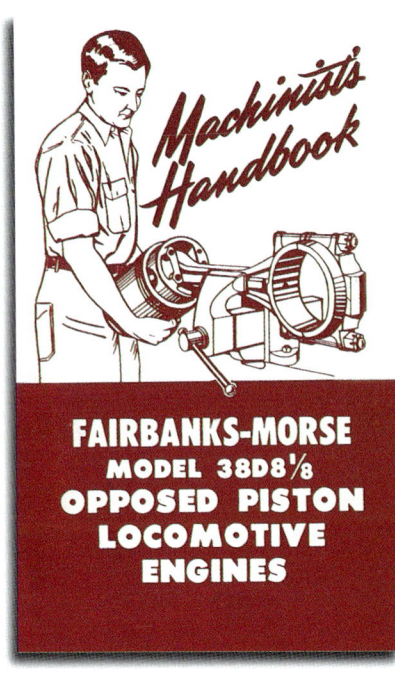

Above ⊕ H-Liner 8554 and CPB16-4 4471 bring an Extra East from Midway by the station at Castlegar, mileage 25.7, on Thursday, August 7, 1969. The tracks to the left of the 1907 station form the wye with the Rossland Sub to Trail and Warfield. In 1898, Montana mining mogul Augustus Heintze sold his Columbia & Western Railway to the CPR. The CPR used the C&W's charter to extend Heintze's Rossland to Robson West line through to Midway by 1900. *(Clayton Jones)*

Below ⊕ N2a 2-8-0 3651 (MLW 7-1910) leads a Mikado on an eastbound double-header about to depart the mining and forestry town of Grand Forks and tackle the 2.4% grade of Farron Hill to the 3,977' summit of the Monashee Mountains. The 3651 was assigned to Nelson in late 1952 and in May 1964 was placed on display in Lethbridge, Alberta.

(Omer Lavallee Collection)

Carmi Sub

On Friday, July 10, 1971, westbound Train 71 is holding at Chute Lake, mileage 106.5 of the Carmi Sub, while en route from Midway to Penticton. The rear brakeman is performing a standing inspection. The 24,000 U.S. gallon water tank a half-mile west of the wye where helpers turned after assisting eastbound trains out of Penticton during the steam era dwarfs the young man. *(Bob Loat)*

Right ⊕ Train 71 is at Arawana, mileage 125.7, in April 1967 and is moving down the 27.2 miles of the Chute Lake Hill that ranged up to 2.2%. Penticton on Okanagan Lake is at mileage 133.7 and was directly accessible by rail when the Kettle Valley Railway building east from Penticton and west from Midway in 1914 was completed at mileage 89.4 on the west side of the Myra Canyon.

(Grant Ferguson, Bill Linley Collection)

Rossland Sub

Left ⊕ Immediately following the end of a strike at Cominco Ltd. in Tadanac, an unusually heavy southbound train descends the 3.6% grade of Poupore Hill north of Genelle, mileage 9.9 en route to Tadanac in July 1972. Enroute back to their normal duties at Tadanac, Train Master 8905 leads 8900 and 8904 replacing the normally assigned 4-axle power. In 1896, the Columbia & Western opened a narrow gauge line from Rossland to access Columbia River steamboats at Trail. By late 1897, a standard-gauged line was in place from Rossland to Castlegar providing a direct connection to the CPR's transcontinental system. *(Stan Smaill)*

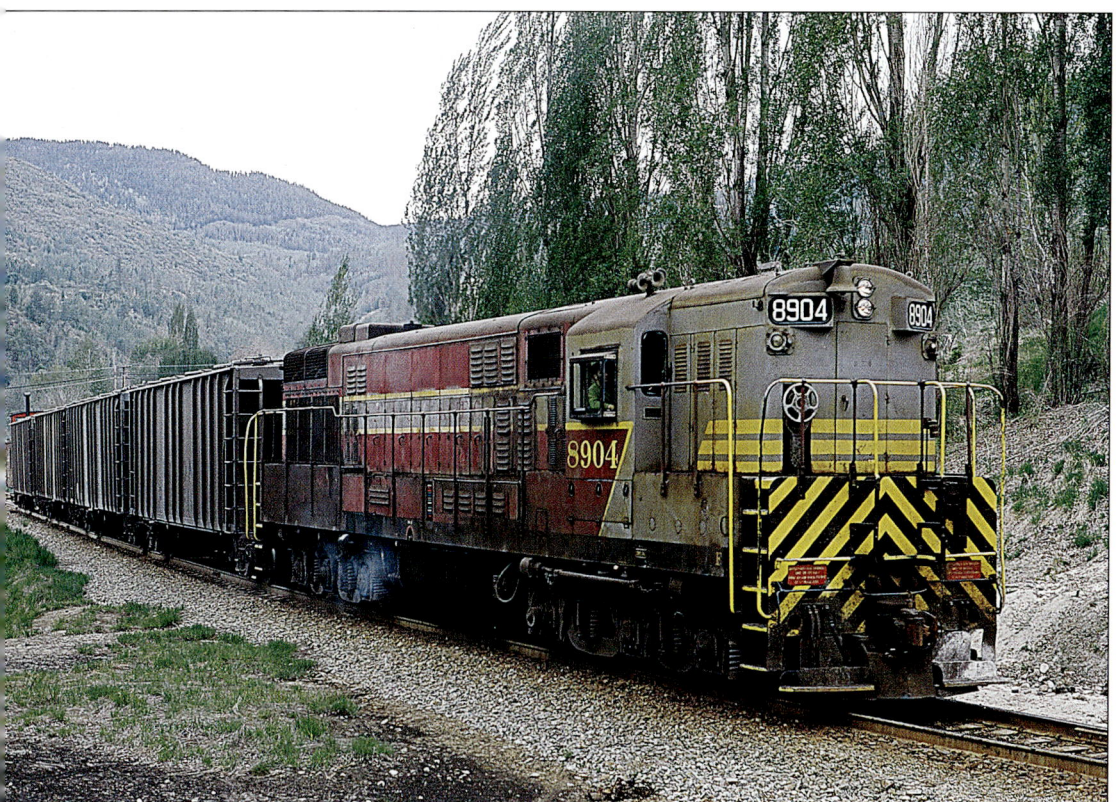

Above ⊕ Trailing a string of phosphate empties, Train Master 8904 is descending the 4.2% grade from Warfield, mileage 21.7 and site of the Cominco Ltd. fertilizer plant on Monday, May 15, 1972.
(Bob Loat)

Below ⊕ Thirty page booklet of January 1, 1959 on train handling.
(Bill Linley Collection)

FORM 583

CANADIAN PACIFIC RAILWAY COMPANY

Canadian Pacific

TRAIN HANDLING
and Other Instructions
Relating to Brake and Communicating
Signal Equipment

Below ⊕ 8905 rests between assignments at Tadanac on Wednesday, September 18, 1968. The Cominco Ltd. plant was owned by the CPR and at the time was the world's largest lead-zinc smelter.
(Bill Linley)

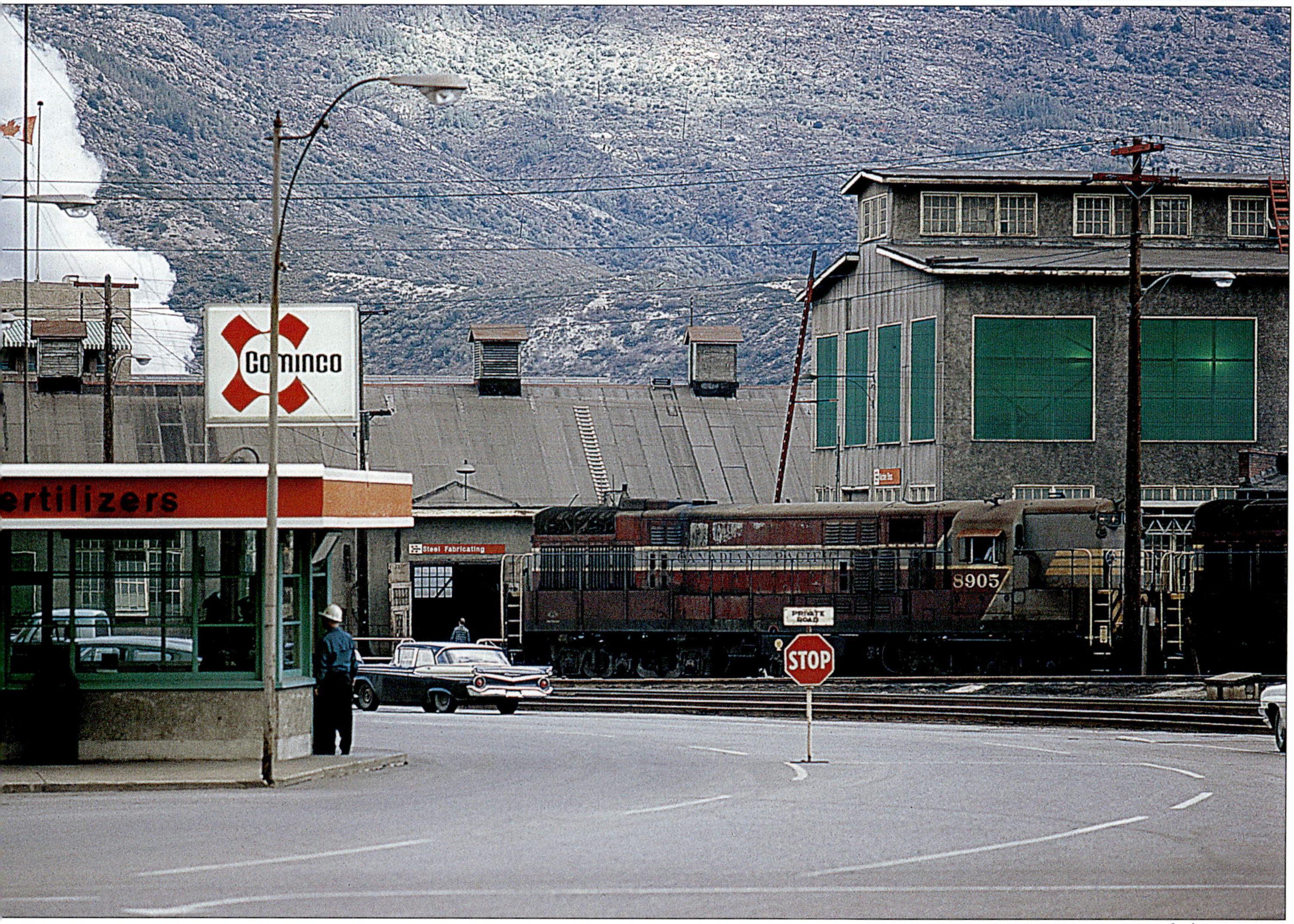

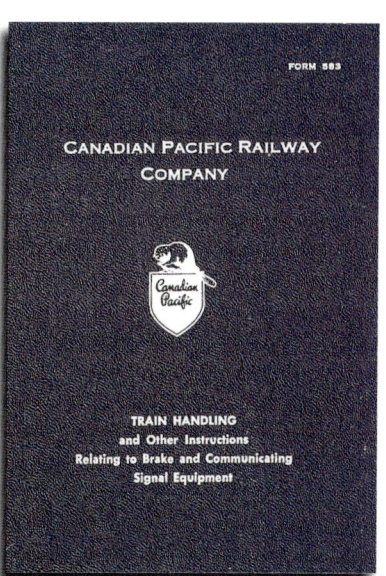

Slocan Sub

Above ⊕ Work Extra 7110, the Slocan Subdivision wayfreight, is homeward bound for Nelson near Beasley, mileage 7.1 of the Boundary Sub on Wednesday September 18, 1968. The DS-10m S-4 was one of six built in the summer of 1952 for the dieselization of the Calgary – Revelstoke mainline; however, they were exchanged for a like number of SW9's and joined the CPR's final four S-4's 7115 – 7118 (MLW 1953) assigned to Nelson Shop for yard and wayfreight service in Southern British Columbia. *(Bill Linley)*

Above ⊕ S-4 7110 stops so that the crew may register in the 1901 station at South Slocan, 11.9 miles west of Nelson on the Boundary Sub. 7110 will set off a pair of loaded chip gons for the mill at Kraft west of Castlegar prior to departing for Nelson on September 18, 1968. The head-pin ore car had come from the mines at Silverton and was barged down Slocan Lake to Slocan City, at the end of track, 31.3 miles north of South Slocan. *(Bill Linley)*

Kaslo Sub

Above ⊕ M4g 2-8-0 3480 (MLW 7-1907) works the barge slip at Rosebery on Slocan Lake on Wednesday, June 17, 1953. From Rosebery, rails extended 40 miles east to the end of track at Kaslo on Kootenay Lake and 26.9 miles west to Nakusp on Arrow Lake.

(Omer Lavallee, R. S. Ritchie Collection)

Arrow Lakes

Right ⊕ Map of the Interior Lakes from a 1950 Public Timetable.

Below ⊕ The 1897 Station at Robson West at mileage 27.4 on the Boundary Sub was on the west shore of Lower Arrow Lake, 1.7 miles west of Castlegar. The ramp led down to the barge slip where the *S.S. Minto* awaits its morning departure for Arrowhead on Tuesday, June 16, 1953. Along the 134-mile voyage, a connection will be made at Nakusp with the 31.2-mile Kaslo Sub that extended to Rosebery on Kootenay Lake. Through passengers enjoyed an overnight stay in Nakusp before continuing to the northern terminus of Arrowhead where mixed Train 801 began its 27.5-mile route to the mainline at Revelstoke. *(Omer Lavallee, R. S. Ritchie Collection)*

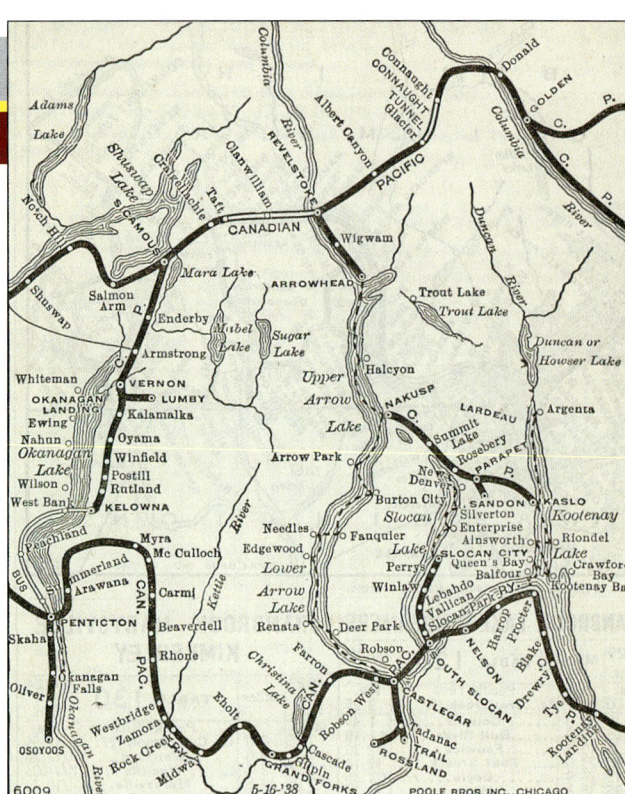

Below ⊕ Freight is being unloaded from the *S.S. Minto* at Nakusp on the afternoon of June 16, 1953. The *Minto* was built in Nakusp, homeport to CPR vessels on the Arrowhead Lakes, in 1898 and was laid-up on April 23, 1954 as passenger service ended, only to be burned in 1968. The latter year also marked the end of service on the Arrowhead Sub as a new dam near Castlegar raised water levels on the lakes.

(Omer Lavallee, R. S. Ritchie Collection)